Future Automation

Changes to Lives and to Businesses

Advances and Opportunities with Big Data and Analytics

Series Editor: Russell Walker *(Northwestern University, USA)*

Advances and Opportunities with Big Data and Analytics

Future Automation

Changes to Lives and to Businesses

Timothy E Carone

University of Notre Dame, USA

NEW JERSEY · LONDON · SINGAPORE · BEIJING · SHANGHAI · HONG KONG · TAIPEI · CHENNAI · TOKYO

Published by

World Scientific Publishing Co. Pte. Ltd.

5 Toh Tuck Link, Singapore 596224

USA office: 27 Warren Street, Suite 401-402, Hackensack, NJ 07601

UK office: 57 Shelton Street, Covent Garden, London WC2H 9HE

Library of Congress Cataloging-in-Publication Data
Names: Carone, Timothy E., author.
Title: Future automation : changes to lives and to businesses / Timothy E. Carone,
    University of Notre Dame, USA.
Description: New Jersey : World Scientific, [2018] | Series: Advances and opportunities
    with big data and analytics ; volume 2 | Includes bibliographical references and index.
Identifiers: LCCN 2016049470 | 9789813142329 (hardback : alk. paper) |
    9789813142336 (pbk. : alk. paper)
Subjects: Automation--Economic aspects. | Technological innovations--Economic aspects.
Classification: LCC HC79.A9 C37 2018 | DDC 303.48/34--dc23
LC record available at https://lccn.loc.gov/2016049470

British Library Cataloguing-in-Publication Data
A catalogue record for this book is available from the British Library.

For any available supplementary material, please visit
https://www.worldscientific.com/worldscibooks/10.1142/10098#t=suppl

Desk Editor: Sylvia Koh

Typeset by Stallion Press
Email: enquiries@stallionpress.com

Printed in Singapore

I dedicate this book to my wife Debbie. For Better, For Worse. For Richer, For Poorer. It is a Team.

Acknowledgements

This book is the culmination of much work over the years and there are more than a few people who deserve thanks. I would like to thank my editors Philly Lim and Yubing Zhai. I would like to thank Russell Walker, Ronald Polidan, Peter Vedder, Jeffrey Hand, and Ian Erridge for early reviews of the book. At various points of our research we benefited from input from Nick Suizzo, Kathy Swain, Tim Walker, Joe Ford, Arlin Wasserman, Ben Reizenstein, and Matt Manzella. TEC would like to thank Dr. Rob Easley, Dr. David Hartvigsen, and Dr. Don Kleinmuntz and the Department of Management at the Mendoza College of Business at the University of Notre Dame for their support. Finally, TEC would like to thank his family and hopes his two sons, Dominic and John, can wait for the next book to have a dedication.

About the Author

Timothy E. Carone, PhD, is an Associate Teaching Professor at the Mendoza College of Business at the University of Notre Dame. Dr. Carone has expertise in autonomous systems, analytics, Internet of Things, and artificial intelligence. He has developed and taught undergraduate, graduate, and executive education courses for Mendoza in the areas of Data Mining, Predictive Analytics, Unstructured Data Analytics, and Emerging Issues. In 2016, he received the Class of 2016 MSBA Outstanding Teacher Award and the Notre Dame Media Legends Award for the Mendoza College. Dr. Carone is a consultant to Fortune 500 companies in the areas of business strategy, enterprise architecture, and key vended technology platforms. He has over 25 years of experience in the design and implementation of high-performance enterprise architectures, the creation and execution of technology strategy projects, and management of complex implementation projects, which have included significant business analytic components. He has leveraged his science and math background to bring sophisticated business analytics solutions to clients and conducted executive training sessions for business leadership on business analytics, data mining, and machine learning. His PhD is in Physics from the University of Arizona. He was a Senior Scientist at the Space Sciences Laboratory at the

University of California, Berkeley, and Staff Scientist at the Lunar and Planetary Laboratory at the University of Arizona. He worked on the Extreme Ultraviolet Explorer satellite, Voyager 1, Voyager 2, and numerous ground-based facilities. He has published numerous peer-reviewed articles on the topics of active galaxies and galaxy formation.

Preface

The World Overstates the Present Fear of Future Risk

Autonomous systems are our future. We do not have much of a choice just as we had no choice when the PC came along, The Internet, the assembly line, electricity, the phone, or other seminal products and processes that induced unwanted but much needed change into our society.

We started looking into the area of automation and autonomous systems over 7 years ago. This was long before the recent explosion in interest on robots and artificial superintelligence. It feels like we have good timing to come out with a book that discusses the impact to business models from automation. This impact is almost a transformation or revolution from our perspective and it feels like our conclusions, while somewhat consistent with other authors and pundits, come at this from a different direction.

We define an autonomous system to be an integration at the data and process level of three components: sensors or the Internet of Things that collect data; big data that stores and processes data; and artificial intelligence, which takes the information, makes decisions, and acts. On occasions, we add in actuators, which are motors that are responsible for moving or controlling a mechanism or system. Other words for an autonomous system with actuators are "robot," "driverless car," and "unmanned drone."

The challenge to the AI component of autonomous system is not to pass the Turing Test. The AI component we portray is not meant to be an artificial general intelligence or artificial superintelligence though they might become one in the process. The AI in this book is a software component; only that can make decisions and act within a narrow context. The speed with which it can do it may make it appear that it is self-aware but this is not the case. The AI will be, for quite some time to come, just a software program running faster and faster. The challenge is for the autonomous system to own and execute a major or mission-critical business process. This context can be a small subset of a business model (e.g., autonomous farm operations to ensure that 100 acres of corn is produced) or very large (e.g., manage a claims process post catastrophe without human intervention). The goals an autonomous system is given must be such that they are achievable in a finite time and have a high probability of achieving or exceeding those goals. Defining goals for narrow tasks is much easier than supporting the goals of business processes that have breadth and depth, like the claims process. Putting an autonomous system in charge of a claims process might be doable but leads to larger challenges.

Can an autonomous system do more than just support rote business processes such as in manufacturing or even driving a car? Can an autonomous system plan strategy? Can it generate innovations? Can an autonomous system create a new startup to disrupt highly regulated businesses like insurance or remittance? At this point the answer is no yet we are moving in that direction as more and more autonomous systems are doing more of the work to support business processes. In addition, until they can do these aforementioned activities, it is difficult to assign meaning to discussions on artificial superintelligence and killer robots that are self-aware.

It is clear that the transition to more autonomous system operating in our society will come from the ground up and will be used to support processes that do not involve humans and human safety. Mostly this falls into the realm of logistics, farming, and some financial services. It does not fall into the area of healthcare where the adoption of autonomous system will be slower and presumably much more highly regulated. Healthcare though will be the place where the human + autonomous system evolves over time and shows how the weaknesses of machines are solved by the strengths of humans and vice versa.

There is one area that can serve as the test bed for autonomous system in other industries. The logistics industry is already highly automated but it can also serve as a test bed for autonomous ports, trucks, planes, and our personal favorite, the Trone, which is a drone that can carry at least as much cargo as a long haul tractor-trailer. If driverless or pilotless logistics modes of transportation have problems, then humans are not in danger as they would be in other industrial areas. If a drone cargo plane crashes in a deserted area, no human is impacted except those disadvantaged by their cargo being destroyed.

There is great fear now mainly due to (1) the danger of artificial superintelligence and (2) the massive loss of jobs due to automation. We are not in agreement with either of these and feel that other options, for now, are available to ensure the transformation, dare we say industrial revolution, benefits humankind.

Will our society be accepting of autonomous system? The foment in the press about the loss of jobs and artificial superintelligence being an existential threat to humanity is not, we believe, where the focus should be. Every change, whether the invention of electricity or the first refrigerators, put people out of work and change our lives to various degrees. There will always be good, bad, and ugly when change occurs. The post-Millennial generation is being born now and they are being raised in the post-iPhone era. To them, talking to Siri or Viv or Cortana will be about as mundane as talking to Mom and Dad. The fact that it took decades of thousands of innovations to get to this point is lost on them just as the centuries of thousands of innovations to get to the car were lost on our generation. As for the artificial superintelligent discussions, we are reminded of the following famous cartoon (by Sidney Harris) which show two mathematicians at a blackboard. A key step in the mathematical proof on the blackboard is the phrase "Then a occurs". Prognostications that artificial superintelligent are an existential threat feels like they use the key step

"I THINK YOU SHOULD BE MORE EXPLICIT HERE IN STEP TWO."

an awful lot in their arguments for superintelligence. For example, most use cases, like the famous paper clip use case, have the superintelligence suddenly acquire common sense from out of the blue.

The post-Millennial generation should find it normal to interact with autonomous systems as if these were other humans. The autonomous systems are not humans but so what. This generation should be OK with embedded IoTs and smart prosthetics. Just as their parents were OK with giving up their privacies on Facebook and LinkedIn, their children will be OK with autonomous systems surrounding them. They will shop online almost exclusively and not need a mall or other physical location to be with their friends or people from other places who are of like mind.

An implicit theme in this book is that the technologies that are being used to field autonomous systems have undergone rapid creation and maturation. That is an artifact of technology development today. The cost of developing new ideas and products is reaching zero thank to things like the Internet, the cloud, and the many platforms that exist to enable rapid creation. This means that many more ideas can be tried, tested, fail, and succeed. The ones succeed undergo further scrutiny and if a critical mass of collective intelligence and innovations are brought forward, these new ideas have the distinct chance of becoming mainstream. This subset of new ideas are in this book. AI has failed many times until now. It has finally reached a stage where the algorithms of past decades can be used due to increases in computing power and the presence of exabytes of data that is of sufficiently high quality that they can be used by the algorithms to create models to operate autonomous systems. The problem is that our ability to incorporate safe and ethical behaviors into these autonomous systems is significantly behind this expansion. In addition, the regulatory framework needed to help properly govern these new technologies is decades old and cannot keep up with the new challenges the platforms present.

Change is coming and it is in many forms and will show up in different places at different times. Our research, presented in this book, attempts to show how this change will show up and is showing up in several industries. This book is written at a point in time and cannot cover all the topics we would like (e.g., the ethics of autonomous systems). It will also be wrong or dated in time given how the change occurs. We believe that what we present will still be relevant thematically. Autonomous systems are clearly operational in agriculture and financial services. The big steps in automation, that mostly show up in logistics first, are driverless cars, trucks, trains, and ports. The maturation of these will then enable these to be used to support human behaviors in commercial transportation. Not too surprisingly, hospitals will remain the laggard except in one area: human + autonomous system interactions. We believe that it is healthcare that will drive the maturation of an intimate human + autonomous system interaction and this, to us, is the most exciting change to come.

May 2018
Cary, IL

Contents

CHAPTER 1

Autonomous Systems

1. What Is an Autonomous System (AS)?

$300 million for 3 milliseconds. That is what Spread Networks paid to lay fiber between New York and Chicago to allow their client's ASs to make billions of dollars. Watson's creator was hired by a large hedge fund to take the next step in developing autonomous trading systems. Google's AS, a driverless car, is well documented, but what is not well documented is how the entire automotive supply chain is slowly changing to support a day when driverless cars are commonplace. The states of California, Florida, and Nevada became the first states to allow driverless cars testing on their roads but are behind the UK and the rest of Europe with driverless car adoption. IBM has spent millions of dollars to create an autonomous health-care system, namely, using Watson to analyze a cancer patient's genome to determine a precise, genetic approach to attacking that person's tumor, an approach that would not work for another person with the same cancer. And the CEOs of banks, insurance companies, logistic providers, healthcare companies, and legal firms have all said that they are really, now, technology companies. Their business processes are becoming automated as is their relationship with suppliers, key vendors, and customers. This automation necessarily involves technology, both hardware and software, and for the first time, an AS is capable of capturing data, interpreting it, and rendering a decision with no human intervention. The shift from humans making all the decisions to machines making decisions has begun.

Autonomous systems define our future. They will become embedded in our lives, much like electricity, to ensure the safety of the food supply. They will become our personal assistant avatar that can do tasks for us during the day, leave us alone when we want, and be there to talk with us when we are receiving a cancer treatment to tell us they agree with the procedure the doctors are performing based on all the research available from the past 60 years. Your avatar might even find another avatar from a cancer patient to talk with you about what to expect.

Autonomous systems will also cause disruptions to existing business models, forever changing how supply chains work and how humans work. Let us take the driverless car as an example. And ask the following question: if driverless cars become ubiquitous, does that change a car dealership, the linchpin for the automotive industry? We argue below that the car dealership business model evolves into a model that resembles a rental car agency but with greater value added. However, rental car agencies will become competitors to dealerships, setting up a major disruption to the customer-facing end of the automotive supply chain. This occurs because if cars drive themselves, consumers would be able to subscribe to a service that sends them the car they need on demand. In the mornings, a car can take you to work and drop you off but in the evening a pickup truck comes for you because you need to haul mulch from the nursery. When you are done with the mulch delivery the pickup truck leaves. Coupled with a mobile app, this sounds like the current services that Uber and Lyft operate with human drivers. Except the human drivers will not be needed in the future.

The presence of ASs could be the nexus for changes of the magnitude experienced during the first and second industrial revolutions. Prior to the 1700s, humans made all the decisions while humans and animals did all the work. Since then, there have been two industrial revolutions that resulted in machines displacing first the animals and now the humans. Humans still made most of the decisions throughout these two revolutions, while the animals were relegated to become part of the human food supply. Now, we are approaching a point where machines will begin to displace humans in the decision-making space. The next industrial revolution can be thought of occurring when machines displace humans from doing the work and from making the decisions. However, we do not think humans will be relegated to some AS "food supply chain" as is popular in science fiction.

So how do we define an AS? It is a term that we started using over 7 years ago when we started to perform research on how these systems will impact business models. We have settled on a definition that is in no way official but was empirically arrived at through our work. An AS is defined to consist of three components and one process. The components are (1) an analytics repository, (2) an artificial intelligence (AI) service, and (3) sensors that generate content, or, as is in vogue, the latter is referred to the Internet of Things (IoT). Robots are ASs with actuators. The process required is a decision-making process that enables the AS to act based on its AI service leveraging the analytics repository that is created with content generated by the IoT.

2. Analytics

The usefulness of ASs will be based on the quality and quantity of the data present to train an AS to be used to support one and eventually multiple processes. Autonomous systems make decisions using data that informs a software program that uses one of the many AI algorithms. AI algorithms are not very complex. The usefulness of an AI program comes from the data used to train it, not the algorithm itself. The work being done now in Deep Learning has reinforced this point. The Deep Learning algorithm is not complex and can be written down in one page or less. It is the petabytes of data that sets apart different implementations. It is the breadth and depth of data about a specific topic (a database of 100 million cats) that is of high quality and complete enough (quantity) to train an AI to recognize cats in any other image taken ever again.

The term "big data" is still out there can mean many things to business and technology practitioners. We define big data as collections of structured and unstructured data in various states of transformation requiring new approaches to data architecture to support any and all business process. The data transformation process takes data in its rawest form as input and produces information for quantitative analysis as its output. It is the size and velocity of the data and transformation process that forces a change to the traditional data architecture. There is no well-defined number that says that you need a big data architecture if your data needs exceed some number of terabytes or petabytes and typically, to make this investment useful for executive decision-making, many terabytes of data appear to be the minimum necessary. This book conflates the term "big data" and analytics because at the end of the day, it is the analytics, i.e., the information that enables decisions to be made, that is most important.

In Chapter 2 we take a deeper dive into analytics. As an introduction, we quantify the idea of data transformation to include a dimension of time, namely, what is the characteristic timescale for the data. This is shown further in Figure 1.1. Data can be relevant for a few seconds (a tweet), minutes (breaking news), or hours (market prices). Data can also be relevant for decades (the map of Chicago streets). However, data that is relevant for many weeks or growing seasons or 1–3 years are not as ubiquitous as the short of very long duration data even though these intermediary data sets from the backbone for an AS. Also, data at different timescales result in different AS capabilities, The challenge to creating and maintaining an AS depends on the quality of the data but also the relevant timescales of the data.

As an example of the gap problem, let's take a look at a farm growing corn and soybeans in Illinois. Illinois is second to Iowa in corn production, but is number one in soybean production. Both states rank in the top 10 when compared to the production of other countries. Therefore, the investment in farm management is substantial, especially in the area of automation. For years, Caterpillar and John Deere have manufactured farm machinery capable of fairly autonomous operations with specific functions in tilling fields, seed

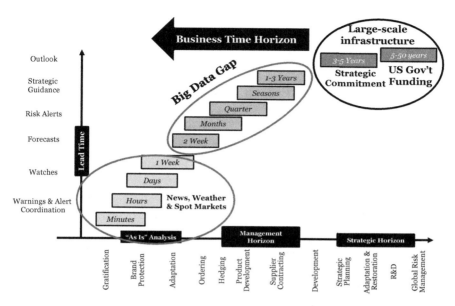

Figure 1.1: The relevancy of data. Data has a useful lifespan ranging from a few seconds to a century. It is the data in the gap that is relevant to ASs and not ubiquitous enough.

planting, fertilization, and harvesting. Putting all this together to completely automate farm management end to end requires an understanding of the fields, weather, seed capabilities, harvesting, futures leveraging, regulations, financing, and so on, that is acquired over time and will be relevant for intermediate periods of time.

This data gap can also be thought of as the data needed to training AS to support business processes that have similar durations. The relevant time horizons for a food company are driven by its new product development and supply chain timescales. Much of that is driven by agricultural processes. A drought is an example of data that is months to years in duration and can be identified with the right types of data. However, this data typically does not show up in the supplier contracting, new supplier development, or strategic planning of a food producer. An AS that supports new product development and supply chain will need this type of data if true farm automation is to be realized as part of a process that supports a food supply chain.

We discuss in detail the most important dimension of analytics, namely, data fusion. Data fusion is the integration of IoT data in its myriad forms, customer data, distribution channel data, machine and human operations data, and partner data. Decisions require a synergistic view of these data. Other important dimensions we discuss are scale and velocity. Cloud architectures have storage that is cheap, and information is free or if it does not exist, less difficult to find or create. Cloud architectures provide enough compute services that processing speed is no longer an economic constraint.

3. Sensors or the IoT

We are surrounded by sensors that document our lives and the rest of the physical world around us. While this has been done to some degree since the invention of the camera, the amount of data collected and the rate at which it is collected provide not just content but now the context within which the content was captured. As with all other technological terms, the word IoT can have many meanings. We extend the use of the term IoT in a McKinsey study.[a] The McKinsey study uses a definition that includes sensors and actuators connected by networks to computing systems. This definition is necessarily a passive collection of data with no overt processing. The definition we adopt for this book is that the IoT includes indivisible physical objects that provide services to the world with which they can share self-generated content, context definition on their surroundings, and interoperate with a larger network of sensors, computers, and networked devices. We include the modifier "indivisible" to prevent collections of IoT devices from being considered an IoT (e.g., a driverless car is an AS to us though some might call it an IoT or even consider it one big sensor).

McKinsey estimates that by 2025, the economic impact of IoT will be in excess of $4 trillion and possibly as high as $11 trillion.

---

[a] McKinsey (June 2015) The Internet of Things: Mapping the value beyond the hype, http://www.mckinsey.com/business-functions/business-technology/our-insights/the-internet-of-things-the-value-of-digitizing-the-physical-world

Much of the value from the IoT will come from business to business (B2B) interactions between IoT devices and not business to consumer (B2C). A key reason for this is that it is in B2B applications that the data generated will find value and not fall on the cutting room floor. The increasing use of data, today estimated to be just 1% of what the IoT generates, is the source of the value and change to business models.

The IoT provides the senses for an AS. With IoT, an AS can capture audio, video, context information, unstructured information, and structured information. The IoT populates the analytics repositories needed to train and operate the AS and can respond to service requests from the AS. There is sometimes an implicit belief that devices in the IoT are not programmable other than to perform their base functions. In the future the miniaturization of transistors, CPUs, GPUs, and other processing elements implies that even for a simple camera, a small circuit board can have a neural network running with significant amounts of data resident. It is this dynamic that drives our definition that an IoT system. It is really a service provider rather than a sensor for passive content creation. The key to getting an AS to work well is to control the data collection process. Therefore, all of the IoT used must be controllable and configurable in an auditable manner by humans and machines. The IoT is the source of value to a business model and is also its worst enemy. We discuss the different classes of IoT and how some of these can be considered to be an AS.

A key component to IoTs are the software platforms built to manage simple and complex networks of IoTs. These software platforms are used as platforms as a service (PaaS). The platforms implement services and micro-services to enable and mange collection and analysis of data from the IoTs embedded in industrial machines and ASs. There are a few of these software platforms available now, such as GE Predix, AWS IoT Core, Azure IoT Suite, AT&T IoT Platform, and IBM Watson. These platforms are as important a decision to end users because they are essentially the operating system for the IoTs that companies use. A company cannot change to another platform once they choose a platform regardless of what vendors say or imply.

4. Artificial Intelligence

We discuss AI in greater detail in the next chapter at a level appropriate for business leadership. As an introduction to that deeper dive, we define AI to be an agent that acts rationally.[1] It acts so as to achieve the best outcome or the best expected outcome given its inputs. These acts can be reflexive in nature or involve inference. An example of the former is that an airplane will always avoid another airplane if the planes get within a certain distance of one another. An example of the latter: as the plane encounters turbulence, it sees other planes in front of it descending 1000 feet. Its analysis of radio transmissions amongst pilots of planes that are descending suggests that they are discussing encountered turbulence. Therefore, in this example, the AI infers that the turbulence is getting worse and can decide to descend without being instructed to by a human controller.

This book adopts the viewpoint that AI will always be about computational statistics and the models derived from improvements in model development. AI software will accrete greater capabilities and speed and that the software will always appear to be intelligent but will never actually be intelligent. AI will never have their own minds or common sense; they will not be self-aware (at least for a very long time). The AI component of the autonomous system discussed in this book is what is always referred to as conforming to the Weak AI hypothesis. A Weak AI model will only at its best simulate intelligence but never be intelligent in the same way that humans are intelligent. AIs will act as if they are intelligent but not have actual minds or common sense. No matter how much words and perspectives describe an AI as being self-aware and sentient, the software will simply be that, software based on computational statistics that is used to created models that can help make decision by human beings or other machines at ever-increasing speeds.

For the foreseeable future, any AI will have narrow capabilities. An AI that can defeat any human or other computer in chess will probably get defeated in a few moves of checkers by a 5-year old whose grandfather spent the better part of an afternoon teaching his grandchild how to play checkers. An AI that is effective for ASs is similarly narrow in scope, and it is important to realize that an

AI trained for one function cannot be repurposed for another function, at least not easily. This will force any AS created to be very narrow in scope as well.

The scope of the AI that we can reasonably expect to see in our future can be categorized according to their capabilities. There are three generally accepted definitions of AS scope:

1. NARROW OR WEAK. These are software programs that can support a process and are the AI that will power an AS as we know them. It is important to note that these systems have no intelligence or common sense. In fact the use of the term AI to describe these is pure marketing. These programs are part of the computational statistics area of study. Chess programs or Siri are good examples of weak AI software, as are the current software that powers the Google cars. For an insurance company, a weak AI can identify claims fraud but not identity theft, another typical offering insurance companies now provide. Companies are still forced to use a specific AI to support a very specific process with well-defined rules. The one aspect of weak AI is that if it performs quickly enough it can fool us into believing that a strong or even artificial superintelligence has been created when in fact nothing of the sort has happened. This was proven out with how IBM Watson was perceived after winning at Jeopardy!

2. GENERAL OR STRONG. We are far from having artificial general intelligence which is software that has cognitive abilities similar to humans and a sense of consciousness. One key problem is articulating the success criteria of when a program has a conscious. A strong AI is typically equated to a human being in most manners of thinking and decision-making. While there are people who have deep domain knowledge across many banking functions, translating their knowledge into a single software program is not feasible at this time. A key impediment is that for a banking SME, what data would be used to train the AI? The knowledge acquired by a single person over 30+ years in banking is unlike the data used to train a Google car. A single person remembers thousands of experiences that help in decision making. It is difficult to encapsulate a life of experiences into terabytes of training data.

3. SUPER. Artificial superintelligence is currently in the realm of science fiction though it gets the vast majority of press coverage due to its existential nature. Super AI is human level intelligence executed a thousand times faster or more. Such a program could create its own economies from scratch, evolve them over time-scales of seconds, be done with them, and then create a new economy a few seconds later. The consensus is that we are decades from such an AI being manifest. And how will the Super AI interact with humans? It will have to and not "ignore" us as if we are the equivalent of ants. If a Super AI wanted to manufacture some product, it would have to work with humans or break the law. This is because some manufacturing will always require a human presence for things like permits and licensing. For example, what if the Super AI required raw materials to be mined in Arizona? It would still need the same permits as Freeport-McMoran Copper & Gold that take more than a few seconds to acquire.

Another challenge for the AI component of a given AS is that this particular AI will be unique because its training data will eventually begin to diverge in content from other identical AS AIs. Take two car AIs, one created in the California Bay Area and one created at Texas Tech University in Lubbock, Texas. The two AIs may be comparable in addressing the basic traffic rules but what about highway driving? Will a car whose AI learned how to function on Interstate 880 be able to operate to a customer's satisfaction on Interstate 27 or the snows of Taos, NM? For the basic traffic laws, there should not be a difference but there will be cultural differences in what makes for a satisfactory driving experience in both places. Can we really expect a car to handle even the basic traffic laws in any region of the country even though the AI was trained based on data from one region? Now one can say that the AI of the car can incorporate different regions of the country and cultural experiences but the problem is not one of technology. People prefer driving their own way which makes them happy. With driverless cars we are now forcing everyone to delight in their car being driven one way and one way only. The cultural assimilation of automation will be a big ask.

Of interest is the recent phenomena of predicting the end of the world from superintelligent computers.[2,3] We would like to say a few words here now to set the tone. There are good reasons to believe that superintelligent systems, namely those that can make decisions thousands of time faster than a human, will one day exist. To deny this is to commit the same error that Ernst Rutherford, the father of nuclear physics, who said that "… anyone who looked for a source of power in the transformation of the atoms was talking moonshine …." After reading the article in *The Times*, Leó Szilárd conceived of the idea of a nuclear chain reaction while walking around London and within a year had filed a patent application.[4]

There are two questions that are being addressed now: (1) when will artificial superintelligent appear and (2) how will they treat humans? However, we do question the time to superintelligence emergence. The latest published estimate[b] shows that the median estimate amongst AI practitioners is that superintelligence will arrive around 2042. This prediction should be considered in the context that in the past, all AI predictions about when some AI capability would arrive have been wrong. A panel discussion of AS professionals[c] discussed the fact that there are significant discoveries yet to be made that need to be in place before artificial superintelligence can be instantiated.

The answer to how AI will treat humans is colored by too much science fiction and is typically accompanied by a picture of the Terminator. There is no reason to believe, a priori, that artificial superintelligence results in an emergent hostility to humans with the innate intent of eliminating us. In fact, there is considerable effort being expended to create a safe AS that would prevent such a future, where superintelligent AS is an existential threat to humans.[5]

---

[b] Katja Grace, http://aiimpacts.org/update-on-all-the-ai-predictions/
[c] Information Technology and Innovation Foundation (30 June 2015) Are super intelligent computers really a threat to humanity?, The video can be found in https://itif.org/media/are-super-intelligent-computers-really-threat-humanity

5. Putting it all Together

What is the "so what" behind the desire to connect everything? What is the "so what" if a baseball is connected to a scorebook? Is that more important than the connection between industrial products? A sensor is any object that generates data regardless of the type of data or how rapidly the data is generated. A sensor can be a temperature sensor, a webcam for pictures and video, a specialized computer chip, a computer model, or a human.

For the decision-making process, we choose the Observe-Orient-Decide-Act (OODA) process made popular by John Boyd. Other decision-making processes can be used here as well though it is not obvious there is much benefit from complicating the process. We expand on the concept and process later on (see Fig. 2.1).

Figure 1.2 shows the OODA process.

The AI service can be a passive or active participant in the OBSERVE phase where sensors collect or generate data at a consistent rate. The AI can decide what data to take or simply take what it is given. This data, which becomes part of one or more data repositories, will undergo some sort of simple to complex processing step.

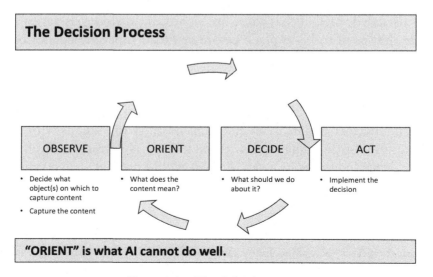

Figure 1.2: The OODA process.

The output from this processing step is an exploitation step that turns the data into analytical information. This analytical information is the output of the OBSERVE phase and is the input to the ORIENT phase. It is in the ORIENT phase where the fastest growth of AI will occur and where AI is currently weakest. It is in this step where the question "what does it all mean" is asked and answered. Right now, an AS service can perform simple tasks here such as identification of a cat in a picture. But right now it cannot look at video data and say "that is a black cat running towards its owner because it is being chased by a large coyote." It will be many years before an AI service is on par with a human being in this phase and is the main reason, as we will argue later, that the most optimal AS is an AI with an analytics repository, sensors, and a human being who owns the decision-making process. This also allows a different perspective on what human labor will look like in the future. Certainly robots,[d] simple ASs, will replace some workers but our research suggests that new types of jobs will be created that are best filled by an AS and a human working as a single entity.

The DECIDE phase can be accomplished by an AI service if it is a rote action. The decision to kill is the most ethically challenging. While it can be straightforward to enable an AI to decide to kill a human or an animal, that action is currently not allowed even in a battlefield situation. The decision to kill is one that requires a human to be in the loop. Other decisions of great importance also require humans. We see this today with such activities as flying a plane or driving a car, for instance. Commercial airliners are highly autonomous in nature; in truth, the pilots do very little other than oversee take-offs and landings. An airliner can do these as well but an airline company that fires all its pilots to do fully autonomous operations would have few passengers as the latter are not yet comfortable with no pilot on board. The role of a human in the DECIDE phase remains, even though automation can accomplish these decisions. In large part this is because we are mostly, unwilling to accept

---

[d] Keep in mind that we define a robot to be an AS with actuators for the purposes of this book.

the error of automated critical decisions (such as taking or risking lives), yet.

The ACT phase is when decisions are implemented. This is an area where ASs excel. A high-frequency trading (HFT) system executes an OODA loop every few hundred microseconds, and it has no human intervention at these speeds. Driverless cars will execute an OODA loop every few milliseconds as it drives down the road and has to deal with stoplights, pedestrians, first responders, and trains. An AS used in an emergency room setting is able to diagnose simple problems at OODA loop times of a few seconds once the patient is hooked up to sensors. More complicated diagnoses and clinical diagnoses still require the expertise of a human being, though it is clear that an AS teamed with a human is a better solution.

We also acknowledge the need for hierarchical ASs. For example, a car driven by a human has over 300 specialized computer chips in it that collect data, analyze and contextualize the data, and may make a decision, that results in an action to pass the data to other chips in the car or directly to the driver display. And the AS may do such actions every millisecond.

6. Current Concepts

We know that the AS will be in our future in a big way. Autonomous systems are already in our daily lives time in small, medium, and increasingly large ways. To most, the existence of an AS in their lives is not apparent. The importance of the AS in our lives will grow by slow accretion of AS capabilities and not a big bang arrival. The future, i.e., the use of AS to support our lives, will appear in different places at different times over the next decade. As equally important to interactions between a human and an AS will be interactions between two or more ASs. For instance, an autonomous car might interact with the ASs of the house, whereby the arrival of the car prompts the system in the house to turn on lights.

In many ways, HFT systems are the most mature AS in existence, today. The AS component of an HFT is growing in importance given the increasing importance of world markets and their associated complexity to trading opportunities. Most trades executed globally in all markets are done by HFTs. Humans are removed. Contrary to popular opinion, HFTs are never turned off or stop trading for very long. HFTs receive data constantly about companies, news reports about economy, business, and conflicts (especially commodity-rich areas), and most importantly, what trades are being executed by whom and on what exchange. As much data as possible is fed into these ASs and they learn better and better ways to trade. The latter has driven the owners of HFTs to reduce the time it takes for the OODA loop to execute. The length of a loop has been decreasing to the point that as of mid-2015, OODA loops (one or more trades) are done in tens of microseconds. It is interesting to watch a given instrument, such as the mini-S&P future, and its trading volume just before a market-moving announcement is made. One sees about 10,000 trades a minute being executed in just this one financial instrument, which implies many HFTs are up and running, trading with one another, waiting for data to be generated from which hundreds of thousands of trades are then executed within a second or two of the news being released. A recent behavioral characteristic being demonstrated by HFTs is an apparent level of cooperation of two or more HFTs. This level of cooperation was not an intended outcome from any HFT designer. Apparently some HFTs are learning that cooperative behavior can help them achieve their goal of maximizing profits.

As mentioned before airplanes are largely autonomous, too. Typically, pilots operate the aircraft from gate through take-off until the aircraft reaches a set altitude. At that point, the autopilot is engaged and the rest of the aircraft systems take over all operations. The pilots, largely, do not get involved again until the aircraft descends through a set altitude and begin flying the plane again. The reason this is effective is that there are strict rules for planes in the air, as agreed to by all countries, such that an airplane and its operations can be codified in an AS. However, this is not the case for ground operations. Right now, it is not possible to provide for complete and reliable ground operations due to the nature of what actually happens on the ground at an airport. The ground operations at an airport include not just aircraft but buses, baggage carts, fuel trucks, security vehicles, de-icing trucks, and so on. Each airport has a ground traffic control system that directs planes to their gates once they have landed and the path they take to the gate depends as much on the availability of gates as it does on the location of ground vehicles. In fact, airport designs that support only fully AS aircraft do not look like any airport we recognize today.

Another class of an AS involves software, such as viruses and worms, attaching computer systems or computer-operated machinery. Generally targets have a significant computer footprint. Of course, this use of an AS in highly controversial and raises legal and ethical questions. This class of AS has much in common with the HFT AS, in that the AS component is becoming more sophisticated as it learns more from previous computer worms such as Stuxnet.[e] The AS component of a worm is learning more and more about infrastructures (e.g., electrical grids, sewer, and water systems, military, first responder behaviors, …) and this data is used to train the AS component to search for specific targets such as Stuxnet did when it looked for programmable logic controllers in a certain configuration. Most worms do nothing other than collect data and observe behaviors of the attacked systems. By attacking systems in a variety of ways, these worms begin to gather the data necessary to determine how best to attack a system when commanded to do so. The assembled knowledge of responses can be used to create an attack vector that not only leverages the weaknesses in the defensive technologies but also the weaknesses in the responses of the systems (and their human operators). In principle, as the real attack proceeds, the worm anticipates the response executed by the defending systems and increases the severity of the attack knowing what the defenders will do next.

7. The Good, The Bad, and The Ugly

It is already difficult for humans to ascertain the reasons why ASs cause problems and how to apportion blame. The flash crash of

---

[e] Stuxnet, https://en.wikipedia.org/wiki/Stuxnet

May 6, 2010 saw the Dow Jones crash almost 9% and then recover all in less than 40 minutes. To this day there is still no consensus of cause and effect, though the U.S. Department of Justice is prosecuting one trader.[f] The sequence of events, the consequeces, and how HFTs participated in this flash crash remains a contentious set of issues. Consider the recent bidding war between two Amazon merchants, each attempting to use algorithms to sell an out-of-print version of Peter A. Lawrence's, *The Making of a Fly: The Genetics of Animal Design.*[6] The highest bid was $23.6 million. This Amazon example turned out to be a harmless. Consider what happens when a driverless car has a failure. The consequence of that failure will challenge the regulatory framework of driving, as well as to how much control we will have over our lives. For example, tinkering with your driverless car could very well be forbidden in the near future due to copyright laws associated with the software present in your car.[7] The auto companies consider the software code to be licensed to the car's owner so the owner cannot change anything. All changes would have to be done by certified mechanics (or coders). In a world of ASs, what does a person control or own? Will they own the appliances in their home? Will they own their home? Will they want to? The answer to the latter will determine the extent to which society allows automation to replace humans.

A given AS will be complex, which is a direct reflection of the process that created it in the first place. The ideation, product development, software development, testing, and deployment processes are becoming less manual and more automated, already. One can envision when the vast majority of the work being done to produce a new car has little or no human intervention. Are we headed for a world in which Fortune 50 companies produce a million cars a year, and have only 31 employees? In a class action suit, who will testify as to the production process that created the buggy software that caused the driverless car to speed up when it approaches a red light?

[f]S Brush, T Schoenberg, and S Ring (21 April 2015) *Bloomberg Technology*, http://www.bloomberg.com/news/articles/2015-04-22/mystery-trader-armed-with-algorithms-rewrites-flash-crash-story

Who will own the liability of such an error? The firm who programmed the car? Probably. Will humans even understand the process that produced the bad software? We ask, because the software might even be generated by an AS. Will a human be able to figure out what the code did (an AS in its own right) to produce the bad software? And how do we know it was bad software and not a normal outcome from the process that trained the neural network that decided to speed up at red lights? We currently examine and judge outcomes with the expectation that a human made a decisions to effect the outcome. Things get turned upside down when the is no human decision involved or the human element is not directly traceable to the outcome.

The pervasive presence of ASs implies a considerable lack of control by humans over their own lives. For example, the cost of health care has resulted in governments and activists trying to exert control over what we eat. The recent effort to ban large sodas in New York City was driven by a desire to reduce caloric intake, especially amongst the young.[8] In a scenario where your employer's health-care coverage mandates that you maintain a certain weight, and you are 50 pounds over that limit, then your appliances might be forced to only store and prepare foods consistent with that mandate. In such an example, The control of your appliances is not with you but with some other entity that is paid a fee by your health-care provider to manage your weight. In this case, the AS, which is your house and its contents, is not controlled or owned by you. The operation of your home could be so laced with software and sensors that you cannot reasonably expect to operate them at all, but simply interact with the system. Another entity controls and manages your home for you (perhaps another AS). The home management systems might get compensated for that by you, the entity that holds your mortgage, your health-care company, your local government, and really a consortium of interested parties. Finally, if the government imposes a carbon footprint on its citizens, then it can ensure that no AS car transports you without evidence that you are providing a carbon offset. Perhaps after driving a certain amount of miles per year, your cost of driving automatically goes up with the premium going to the government. The government has the ability to enforce policies now at the level of the AS without your approval or permission. Automation will be an effective tool for government.

People may also lose control of their online presence and access due to the operations of multiple ASs. Currently, online advertisements are important to companies that are selling apps and other content and services to users of tablets and smartphones. In 2016, it is expected that total mobile advertisement spend will be $100 billion and for the first time will account for more than 50% of all digital ad expenditure[g]. When people click on an adverstisement, the app or website they are using sends them to the advertiser's app or website and the advertiser receives information from the sender about the person and pays a fee to the sender. For example, Facebook, which derives over 70% of its revenues from mobile advertisements, provides, back to the advertiser, precise information about customers who click on an advertiser's mobile advertisement. However, Facebook can, if it wants, deny that information to advertisers and insist that in return for sending them this precise information, the advertiser share all of their customer information with Facebook, even if those customers don't have a Facebook account. [9] Over time, Facebook, Google, and other social media sites can continue to enrich the information about a person to such an extent that they will own the most complete digital profile of a person in existence. The like of Google and Facebook will do this using ever-increasing sophisticated ASs. It is not much of a stretch to imagine how companies, banks, and indeed even the government could go to a social media and learn a lot about you, because the AS that created that data is authoritative, complete, and does not need your permission for access. Multiple ASs can share information about you to meet their needs without your knowledge. It raises questions such as who owns the data created by an AS? Most likely (if not certainly) the owner of the AS does.

---

[g] Mobile Ad spend to top $100 billion worldwide in 2016, 51% of digital market, 2 April 2015, http://www.emarketer.com/Article/Mobile-Ad-Spend-Top-100-Billion-Worldwide-2016-51-of-Digital-Market/1012299

8. Levels of Autonomous Systems — How it Begins to Show Up

There are a number of ways to relate the degree of autonomy in a system. We forward the categorization shown in Table 1.1. The categorization ranges from Level 0 where there is little or no presence of an AS (and significant human involvement) to Level 5 where there is no human presence at all, or if there is some human involvement, it is passive as in a human utilizing an otherwise AS, which is in complete control. This categorization is further refined later in this book by considering the relative maturity of the use of ASs through major components including: the use of analytics, and the role of sensors. These components relate the breadth and depth of how an AS supports or directly executes business processes.

Table 1.1: The Levels of Autonomy used in this book to categorize an AS and its relative use of AS, analytics, and sensors.

Level of autonomy	Definition	Examples
0	The human has full control over the AS.	Bicycles, sports
1	The AS has some features that temporarily take control from the human for timescales that are shorter than human abilities.	Automobiles, claims processing, farming, autopilots, order fulfillment
2	The AS has some features that temporarily take control from the human for timescales that are shorter than or the same as human abilities.	Automobiles, aircraft, manufacturing, news article creation
3	The AS has control and the human augments operations in the case of problems or other reasons.	HFTs Space shuttle
4	The AS has complete control and there are minimal roles for the human.	The automobile in 2025? Farms by 2025?

Today we live with ASs that are at Level 1 and 2, and there is a level of comfort associated with these ASs because we find them useful, and they can exist within our existing regulatory frameworks. Many schools use GameChanger for people to use in following a baseball game regardless of their location. When the game is over, GameChanger uses an AS program to automatically write and publish a news copy of the game tailored for the customer. For example, the story of a game will emphasize the accomplishments of one team, namely the team the customer is following, or a player of special interest. The story of the same game published to a customer who follows the other team will read differently and emphasize the accomplishments of the other team. This allows GameChanger to provide the content that is most important to the reader. It is customized news (or entertainment) for the reader, and it is generated through an AS.

One other impact of the adoption of ASs involves reliability. As we implement more sophisticated levels of automation, human interaction (and error) pose an increased threat to the level of system reliability. In short, humans need training on how to use advanced ASs, too. This challenge to reliability will begin to show up as the majority of the ASs in our society start to move from Levels 1 and 2 to Levels 3 and 4, requiring a new behavior by humans. There is already evidence that as the AS does more of the work and the human less, it becomes more difficult for the human to successfully take over the AS operations. For example, a number of aircraft incidents, in recent years, have been linked to the failure of integration between the autopilot system and its pilots, when challenging situations arise. The handoff from an AS to a manunaul one, in a rapidly changing situation can disorient the pilot because of the need for the pilots to ORIENT themselves. In these tragic airplane examples, the pilots made poor decisions because they did not understand the true problem and were not OBSERVING the systems (owing to the reliance on the autonomous operator). We should expect that accidents tied to this dynamic of humans intervening in automation will increase in occurrence in cars and other ASs used regularly by humans over the next 10 years. The handoff from an AS to a human during a crisis will require special attention.

9. Optimal Autonomous Systems? Think Autonomous System and a Human

In 1960, Licklider wrote a key paper titled "Man–Computer Symbiosis," where he argued that man and computer will enter into a cooperative interaction.[10] Over the subsequent 50 years, the topic he raised is very relevant and, in fact, may hold the key to not repeating the massive societal displacements experienced in the first and second industrial revolutions.

Humans were successful during the transitions of the first and second industrial revolutions because they repurposed themselves to operate the new machinery instead of competing with the machinery. Men and eventually women left the ploughs in the field and learned how to participate on assembly lines, operate heavy equipment, and drive locomotives. Productivity was increased by putting machines in the control of humans. These new machines could not make decisions and still needed human operators. Eventually these machines began accreting the capabilities to perform the most rudimentary of decisions and, like the automatic transmission in a car, had analog components (and even rudimentary computing devices) that could reliably perform their tasks in creating the new societies of the eighteenth, nineteenth, and twentieth centuries.

The increasing rate with which digital technologies are overtaking analog technologies has further increased efficiencies in business, allowing humans to be deployed with control over larger systems. The best example is that of a telephone switchboard operator. AT&T once employed over 100,000 people as operators. As technology improved, fewer and fewer operators were needed, as increasingly intelligent digital techonologies, provided greater capabilities, allowing fewer operators to do the work once done by many. It is estimated today that if AT&T still supported its network with human operators, they would need well over 1 billion employees, which shows that the old analog and manual switch networks were not scalable. Automation and digitization were demanded in order to achieve efficient scale. There was a further upside to the repurposing of the operators. Repurposing the operators, allowed them to pursue higher valued work in the information economy. It also reduced the mundane, repetitive, and often dangerous work done by humans. Today, we have arrived at a point, perhaps a tipping point, where machines possess a powerful assembly of capabilities that include ASs, and access to data and analytics, while also providing control over hydraulics and actuators and a myriad of components. This is all made possible through a digitization made possible by computers, sensors, and wireless networks. Such advanced machines can do more of what a human does. These machines can now compete with humans on decision-making and value judgments instead of strictly manual work. In other words, machines are performing at a level so closely commensurate with humans that it is now estimated that up to 47% of jobs that exist in the United States today will be done by ASs in the next few decades.[11] Many rote processes, such as manufacturing, are being performed by robots. Over the next few decades, ASs will begin replacing journalists, health-care workers, scientists, engineers, and other very skilled workers whose work processes involve more ORIENT functions. These encroachments will be examined in Part 2 of this book.

The advantage for humans seems to be in the ORIENT phase of the OODA loop. If policy evolves to require or protect the role of human in a process, we can expect that certain DECIDE and ACT processes (such as firing a weapon) will also remain within the purview of humans. Largely, it will be a social and legal choice. Autonomous systems can and already do perform DEDICE and ACT processes. Undertaking the work analysis data and determine its meaning in a context is the most difficult process an AS can perform. Excellence in this analysis requires experience. Humans develop this experience innately through our memory processes. Autonomous systems must build such repositories of knowledge from experiences, too. This involves training the AS on content and context, which implies that the data required in training must provide a sufficient breadth and depth of knowledge required to consider a set of decisions and take action. This training process mirrors the development of human knowledge in many ways.

Removing humans from the regular decision-making process introduces a new risk. We, as humans, are imperfect operators, benefiting from practice, familiarity, and repetition. As we rely on ASs for more, we can also expect deterioration in human skills, owing to the less regular exercise of those skills. This risk is especially problematic in the transition from human decision-making to AS decision-making. As ASs take over more of the work for humans, humans will need to focus on different things. However, the AS will not be of sufficient skills that it can deal with all problems. Humans will be required for special cases. Recognizing those cases and being ready to act will be the new focus and responsibility of humans. We expect a transition phase in the evolution of automation. In this phase, humans to AS interaction will be critical. Humans will even need specialized training on what to do when the system needs human help. There will be a time when the AS malfunction will require the intervention of humans. We examine this important interaction between humans and ASs in Chapter 4, Section 4.

10. Overview of Business Impact

Assessing how an AS will impact a particular business model requires understanding the different parts of a business will be impacted. We approach this through a framework that examines the impacts to the business model, as shown in Figure 1.3.[h] It has the following components:

1. Customer Facing

    a. Customer Segment. Defines customers based on a consistent set of attributes.

---

[h] A Osterwalder, Y Pigneur, A Smith, and 470 practitioners from 45 countries (2010). *Business Model Generation*. Self-published.

b. Customer Experience. Defines the nature and outcomes of the interactions between a business model and its customers.

c. Distribution Channels. Defines how the value proposition is delivered to the customer segments.

2. Value Proposition

a. Core Offering. The key and defining product or service offered by the business model to its customer.

b. Complementary Offering. These are adjacent offerings that complement the core offering and are most subject to change induced internally and externally.

c. Brand Strategy. Defines the value proposition or promise in the product or service.

3. Enabling Capabilities

a. Core Processes and Resources. The basic processes that ensure a business can operate.

b. Enabling Processes and Resources. The use of resources to deliver a product or service.

c. Value Creation Partners. These are external entities that provide additional value to the overall business model.

4. Cost Structure

a. These are the fixed and variable costs associated with operating the business model. The fixed costs are driven mostly by the cost of the Enabling Capabilities and the variable costs depend on how well the value proposition and customer-facing components are managed.

b. The cost of adopting new technology is captured here. Careful consideration is needed here. Not all technology lowers cost. For instance, going to the cloud may actually drive up the cost of IT operations, even though the expectation is that over time this cost flattens out or its increase is slower than the increase in net new revenues from changes to the business model.

c. Businesses cannot operate without internal financial processes and controls, and basic supply chain processes. These processes reduce operational risk and a very much required in a modern business. These processes are ripe for automation.

5. Revenue Streams

    a. The impact of automation to business models is considered here. Ideally, automation yields new revenues. Much of the revenue for companies leveraging automation will be "new," meaning they are will originate from these new automated business capabilities rather than from augmented current capabilities. Other current capabilities will migrate from the front to the back of the business model (such as the role of a salesman being displaced by an algorithm of set of web services).

We acknowledge that the business model in Fig. 1.3 is not complete. However, for the purposes of our analysis, it provides the key learnings that demonstrate how pervasive the use of AS in businesses will be over the next few decades.

11. A Word about Platforms

A growing trend is that ASs will be delivered as platforms rather than a software package or a combination of hardware and software.

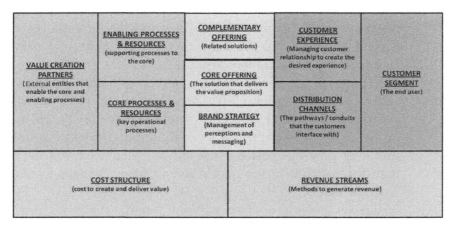

Figure 1.3: A representation of a business model.

What is a platform? As is the case in the world of technology, it means many things to many people. The definition we adopt for the book is that a platform is a structure that allows the creation, support, and evolution of connected personal and business capabilities. Platforms are delivered using a service model and are typically built on cloud infrastructure even if the platform itself is not delivered via the cloud. There are traditional platforms such as AWS Elastic Beanstalk, Google App Engine, and Apache Stratos. However, it is less apparent that Facebook, LinkedIn, Google Search Engine, and Salesforce are also platforms in that they enable business capabilities to be created and managed. The challenge faced is that the platform providers really do not understand how people and organizations will use their platforms. This is why so many were caught off-guard with fake news, election intrusions, horrific videos, and a myriad of other unexpected uses.

A pitfall with the nomenclature is that it is possible for some software vendors to rebrand their software products as platforms when in fact there has been no change to the product. A rose by any other name is still a rose so it is important to carefully differentiate between a true platform that provides evolutionary capabilities from a traditional software product.

12. Summary

The presence of ASs is already changing our lives and business models forever. In effect, a third entity is now present. Whereas, businesses were made up of humans and machines with humans making the decisions, now can expect a future in which businesses are made up of machines interacting other with machines, that also make the decisions. Clearly, humans should have a role in making those decisions that machines cannot currently make. However, the scope of those decisions reserved for humans will slowly decrease with time, as automation advances.

The nature of machines is changing. The addition of ASs, the creation of analytics repositories, and the IoT allow machines to shed their human masters, even when executing complex business processes. Leveraging the data collected from the IoT to make informed and contextualized decisions will allow ASs the ability to compete with humans in decision-making. As the knowledge base of experiences increase, through training, we should expect the scope and complexity of the process enabled by ASs to grow until the most mission-critical processes are under their control.

In the next three chapters, we take a deeper dive into important components of ASs: nalytics, artificial intelligence (AI), and the Internet of Things (IoT). Each of these components of the AS will impact businesses. We assume that ASs use wired or wireless capabilities as needed, and adoption communication capabilities such as voice recognition and image processing that continue to mirror human decision-making processes.

Part 2 of this book provides details on the impact of ASs business model, with special consideration given to the domains in which the AS will operated. The tools and considerations described above are used to perform this assessment, further allowing consideration of the breadth and depth of changes to business models when ASs arise in specific domains.

The research we have undertaken leads to the conclusion that the development of ASs will significantly disrupt most, if not all, business models in existence. Overall, most businesses will reach Levels 3 and 4 of automation maturity over 1–2 decades. In these advanced levels, many the mission-critical processes will become automated along with other core and enabling processes, including back of house and vendor interactions. These changes will not be apparent to the general public themselves as discrete changes but, instead, will be manifested through derivative changes, as seen in the evolution of the driverless car. Modern car show elements of automation, including automated parking, change lane assistance, and sensor controlled braking. This gradual inclusion of autonomous sytems will continue in all forms of business. Autonomous systems are beginning to appear more overtly in customer management and measuring customer experience. These changes will be driven by better use of analytics to better serve the customer. Expect the integration of voice recognition, and mass customization solutions to become the norm.

All of these will be driven by autonomous process, not direct human interactions.

The deep-learning algorithms that will use the analytics created by systems of sensor will also fill in key knowledge gaps in businesses. Consider the challenge of long-term weather forecasting that is precise and localized. Such forecasting will benefit from many sensors and greater analytical consideration of data sets, created from ASs. The value of greater precision in long-term forecasts is being achieved already as power utilities can develop probabilistic models that identify power lines at risk of damage, with a 3–4 month horizon. Sensors and the automated consideration of analytics are making this possible. Together, the system is behaving more like an AS. The IBM Deep Thunder project is another example of a data set that is creasing the explanation of long-term weather outcomes.[i] Deep Thunder can currently provide weather predictions, including wind velocities at a specific Olympic diving platform, with a 3–4 days horizon. Such precision with such a forecast periods was never possible before. Just a few years ago, the Deep Thunder predictions were only accurate within a few hours. The ability to measure more aspects of weather and consider those aspects through deep-learning is changing how can plan for the future. Such forecasts can clearly be used in logistics and business operations to plan for disruptive (or favorable) weather.

Another and equally as important data gap to be filled will be seen in the prediction of food production. Precision agriculture practices and remote sensing technologies now exist to count and manage every corn stalk and soybean plant in the United States using small drones. This same technology can also monitor the health of every one of those plants and over time, and therefore, provide an increasingly accurate yield estimates. Fusion of the data from all farms on a daily basis is possible. An AS monitoring the farm could provide a crop planting down to the plant level, the amount of crop can be harvested along with location and timing, send notifications

---

[i] IBM, Deep Thunder, http://www-03.ibm.com/ibm/history/ibm100/us/en/icons/deepthunder/

to the USDA on growing conditions, and update buyers on the supply of crop. Sensors embedded in livestock will track the growth of animals, making optimal decisions in the management of livestock possible. The analytics created by this network of sensors will enable ASs for the production of poultry, pig, cattle, and other animal protein sources.

Autonomous systems appear in business supply chains today and their capabilities will continue to increase. The food supply chains are expected to experience automation at a rapid pace in the coming years. The automation of the farm will reduce inefficiencies, and require less human labor. Better long-term weather data allow better planning for climate change. Real-time crop data will allow better food production predictions, which will allow better supply-demand matching, which will ultimately control volatility in food prices. Automating the food processing and food production is underway. More and more humans will have a smaller role in the production of food, giving up more of the work to machines and ASs.

It is becoming more evident that one of the most overt disruptions from automation will be seen in the automobile industry. The customer experience and relationship with cars will change. Driverless cars should induce efficiency changes that will result in far fewer cars being produced every year. In fact, the ability of 3D printers to produce car configurations on demand leads to scenarios where cars can be produced at a dealership based on customer demand. If a dealership can print any part it needs, what value will assembly plants and the Tier 1 and 2 companies provide? Driverless cars will significantly benefit from long-term data that is already in place, such as digital data on roads and other infrastructure. This data generally changes at a slow rate. The data accumulated en masse by millions of driverless cars, each engaged in a single activity such as the morning and evening commuting patterns in major metropolitan areas, will result in a valuable repository of data that can lead to new paradigms for rise sharing, car sharing, trip scheduling, and even road use taxation. Most certainly, the autonomous vehicles will use this data over time to predict the best times for a person to leave their house in order to arrive at a destination based on learned patterns of traffic.

Financial services and legal services are becoming more automated. The former has HFT, which is already a dominant force in financial markets, and the latter is benefiting from document assembling and knowledge discovery. The use of smart contracts in financial exchanges, insurance contracts, and many other transactions of trade can now be well-defined, executed, and enforced with automated processes. Financial services and legal services have collecting high-quality data for such a long period of time, suggesting that the data gap needed to overcome for ASs is smaller than seen in other industries. This strength of data evident in HFTs and will become critical as automation evolves in other aspects of financial and legal services. Robo-advisors, recently made available by some wealth management firms, are just the beginning of automation in financial services. This trend marks the migration of AS and analytics to a broader part of the mission-critical business processes. Retail-banking is a great opportunity for automation. A robo-advisor represented by a human-like avatar can appear on demand whenever needed to carry out the needs of a person, whether consumer or business, helping with transaction processing to loan acceptance. The Millennial Generation shows great comfort and trust with such automation, and that generation grows its wealth, it will look to leverage robo-type advisors for most if not all of their needs.

The biggest barrier that appears to be in place to govern AS adoption is human impedance. A recent report[12] on a survey of 384 Iowa farmers showed that 94% of the respondents used yield monitors, 74% used auto steer, 36% use variable-rate planting, and 34% used field-specific weather data. The majority of farmers reported that the complex integration of all the automation as a major reason for lack of adoption of the more sophisticated automation capabilities. Their concerns are eerily familiar to those of business units and IT organizations from the past 25 years, and it is perhaps comforting that since the latter were able to overcome the biggest integration problems, so too will new cohorts of advanced technology users.

The other expected barrier to AS adoption will be local, state, and federal governments. Autonomous system adoption will cause dislocation to work forces, tax revenues, policies, public safety, and many other areas that governments feel responsible for now and in the future. Their actions will necessarily be reactive in nature and attempt to slow down and change how AS are adopted in the various business domains. The best leading indicator we have is how slowly the government has been developing policies around the use of drones. Policing the use of drones is difficult and as the capabilities of these drones increase, the more difficult it will be for governments to maintain any semblance of order in their use. Right now, most uses of drones are benign though it is not a far leap to imagine hunters using them or for those engaged in illegal activities to leverage drones as protection against first responders.

We conclude this chapter with a description of what we think is the biggest risk of ASs with artificial general intelligence. We use the above definition of artificial general intelligence. There is a mode for which artificial general intelligence can be instantiated and pose a risk to humanity. Consider the decision-making process: OODA, which we discussed above. This process can be optimized at any speed through the combination of human and AS. Both have their strengths and weaknesses relative to one another. The human excels at the Orient and complex Decide phases while the AS can Observe and Act much faster and react faster than a human. A human trained to use an AS that can observe and act based on the ability of the human to make the complex decisions can have two impacts, one difficult and one catastrophic.

The difficult impact is that the combination can own complex processes such as found in supply chains, financial services, and logistics. The combination might even replace large swaths of middle management. The more rote management processes, the easier the combination can replace the humans that support the processes. A reasonable extrapolation of this idea is that much of the Fortune 1000 companies will find themselves being run by fewer and fewer people. Can we imagine Allstate with its 40,000+ employees being run with 1000? Can we imagine McDonalds being run by less than 5000 where now it takes 400,000+? Or Walmart being run by less than 10,000 people rather than the 2.2 million employees it currently has globally? The impact of the human and

AS is that the efficiency of the human increases significantly. They can get more done on their own because much of what they do is routine and rote. The AS can perform much of these faster and without interactions with other humans that would normally result in delays. When a combined human and AS interact with another human and AS, it is reasonable to expect the interaction to be faster and impactful than the incessant meetings we have all been subject to in our professional lives. We are seeing the beginnings of this already with Instagram being taken over by Facebook for $1B with only 13 employees. The advances in technology allowed far more to get done than even in 2000 when Instagram would have needed more software developers and other to produce a similar product.

The catastrophic impact is that a human and AS can also operate a military with far fewer people than exists in most militaries today. Our world has a penchant for creating humans of good and of evil. Evil takes many forms, from the unethical to the megalomaniac. The former is difficult to address as one person's unethical behavior is another's positive behavior. Who is to say? It is the megalomaniac that is the existential threat. Autonomous weapons are reality and will become more autonomous and more effective with time. Large parts of the military forces of a nation-state or a terrorist organization will eventually be replaceable by cyber weapons and robots. A cyber attack can be run effectively by an AS only with no human intervention. Military weapons systems (tanks, artillery, planes, submarines, surface ships, ...) can become fully autonomous over time though the more complex weapons systems will require human direction for quite some time. Just as with Instagram or major corporations, a military should eventually consist of far fewer humans than today. A government with a few humans and a few ASs can govern and execute a foreign policy at greater speeds than their adversaries. Any government that can execute their OODA phase faster than their adversaries will probably defeat that adversary whether on the battlefield or diplomatically. It would be similar to a chess grandmaster playing against a good chess player who has not had much tournament experience.

This scenario becomes existential when the dictator is a megalomaniac. Such a leader could execute a rapid capture of land or some valued asset so that the rest of the world might be able to react in time even with their own ASs. How would the world react? If the megalomaniac has an AS, then so should other world leaders. Each of these ASs will be different because their origin will be in that country's culture and belief systems. The AS a US President would use will have similarities and differences to those used by the leaders of England and Germany. Depending on how much autonomy an AS has in each of the countries, the reaction of each will have similarities and differences. Some might stand down their forces because of a country policy to not further inflame the problems. Others would go to a stronger defense posture and possibly taken reactive and pre-emptive actions as well. The humans in the loop may or may not be able to keep these actions reasonable. Also because it is machines being destroyed and not many humans, it is difficult to assess how public opinion will react to these scenarios which resemble the video games of today.

At what point will it become clear that ASs have reached the point where they are capable of the above operations? Right now ASs can play chess but the same AS cannot play checkers, bridge, poker, and other complex games. We believe that the first indication of the presence of artificial general intelligence being present in ASs is when it can become proficient in all these games. It might be that the first version is a program which is a glorified interface into all the AI systems that can each play a single and different game. It will still be limited but would be strong in all that a game that mattered, not all the games. This is a key point — an artificial general intelligence just needs to be good enough in those high valued areas for the above discussion to be instantiated. It does not have to be able to do everything, just those things necessary for it to execute complex processes such as running a supply chain or leading an insurance company. Autonomous systems with artificial general intelligence should grow by accretion of capabilities; in other words, from the bottom up. This implies that recognition of their existence might be far later than their presence.

References

1. Stuart, R and P Norvig (2009). *Artificial Intelligence: A Modern Approach,* 3rd Ed. New Jersey: Prentice Hall.
2. Eric, M (28 January 2015). *Forbes/Tech.* http://www.forbes.com/sites/ericmack/2015/01/28/bill-gates-also-worries-artificial-intelligence-is-a-threat/
3. Nick, B (2014). *Superintelligence: Paths, Dangers, Strategies,* 1st Ed. Oxford: Oxford University Press.
4. Szilard, L (28 June 1934). Improvements in or relating to the transmutation of chemical elements, http://worldwide.espacenet.com/publicationDetails/biblio?CC=GB&NR=630726&KC=&FT=E&locale=en_EP
5. Brundage, M (2014). Limitations and risks of machine ethics. *Journal of Experimental & Theoretical Artificial Intelligence,* 26(3), 355–372.
6. Murphy, D (23 April 2011). Amazon algorithm price war leads to $23.6-million-dollar book listing, *PC Mag.* http://www.pcmag.com/article2/0,2817,2384102,00.asp
7. William, R (8 July 2015). Auto makers try to stop the gear heads, *Wall Street Journal.*
8. BBC News (13 September 2012). New York City bans supersize sodas, http://www.bbc.co.uk/news/world-us-canada-19593012
9. Dean, T and M Marshall (9 July 2015). Facebook's planned customer-data change called 'land grab' by publishers, *VentureBeat.* http://venturebeat.com/2015/07/09/facebooks-planned-customer-data-change-called-land-grab-by-publishers/
10. Licklider, JCR (1960). Man-Computer symbiosis. *IRE Transactions on Human Factors in Electronics,* HFE-1, 4-11. http://groups.csail.mit.edu/medg/people/psz/Licklider.html
11. Frey, C and M Osborne (2013). *The Future of Employment: How Susceptible Are Jobs to Computerisation?* Oxford: Oxford Martin School. http://www.oxfordmartin.ox.ac.uk/publications/view/1314
12. Iowa Farm Bureau (18 December 2014). *Iowa AgState Big Data Report.* https://www.iowafarmbureau.com/Article/Iowa-AgState-Big-Data-Report

CHAPTER 2

Analytics

1. Overview

The last few years has seen the prominent rise of the field of analytics, a practice that has existed for far longer. Concomitant with this rise is the phrase "Big Data". What is Big Data? We all know what data is, namely, structured data managed in databases like customer information, financial information, and sales. This data conforms to the rules of relational data models.[1] Then there are the unstructured data sources. Approximately 80% of the world's data is unstructured, that is data that does not conform to relational database principles. It is growing at fifteen times the rate of structured data. Unstructured data includes corporate e-mails, financial filings, customer feedback, blogs, online reviews, instant messages, tweets, pictures, videos, and graphs, among others. Extraction of insights from unstructured data is increasingly viewed as a high-valued opportunity but is still a nascent area within many companies and other organizations.

So what does "Big" mean? Details behind what "Big" means can be found elsewhere.[2] For the purposes of this book, we take "Big" to mean "valued" and not "size." Big data can be a few MBs in size or a few PBs. The question is less about size and more about how much actionable information is contained in the data. The total amount of data that has been returned from the two Voyager

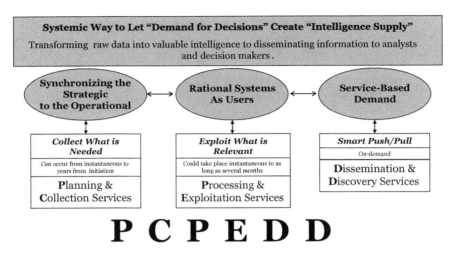

Figure 2.1:   The process to turn raw data into valuable intelligence.

spacecraft are highly valued and total less than a terabyte in size.[a] Thousands of peer-reviewed papers have been published using this data and it has revolutionized our understanding of the Solar System.

What is important is less about how much data is present than what is done with the data. Figure 2.1 shows the process to turn raw data into actionable intelligence. We have known for decades how to execute this process and like many other things we have continually rediscovered what we already knew when new technologies and cultural changes occur. The most important part is the Planning Phase where the decision is made what data to use and how to collect it. Decisions here will dictate what data to collect and from where, how much data preparation will have to be done, what frequencies to collect the data, and what the policies are that govern it all. Another aspect to this is who owns the data, meaning who has the final decision on what happens with the data. This is a more difficult issue than might be evident. One of the most contentious issues at many companies is who owns the customer, meaning who

[a] NASA JPL, Voyager — The interstellar mission, http://voyager.jpl.nasa.gov/mission/didyouknow.html

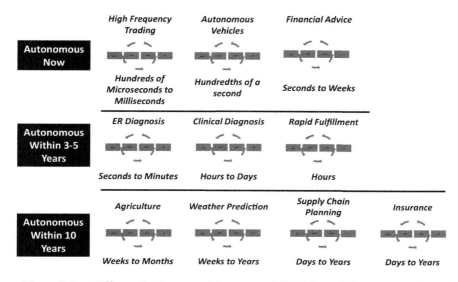

Figure 2.2:   Different business models execute PCPEDD at different timescales.

decides how to manage the customer and is responsible for the data. Unfortunately, many areas of a company think they own the data and customer, and this has resulted in a balkanization of the customer data.

There needs to be an approach to developing analytics, that is, going from collection of raw data to actionable information, that is consistent with the Boyd Cycle (see Figure 1.2). Figure 2.2 is a process we developed, used, and refined over the past decade. We refer to it as the PCPEDD process for Planning, Collection, Processing, Exploitation, Dissemination, and Discovery. The idea is that the need for decisions needed by the autonomous system requires a supply of information or intelligence (aka actionable information). PCPEDD is used to collect the data that is needed to create actionable information and deliver to those actors that need to use the intelligence to make a decision and carry out the decision. The PCPEDD process is described further below.

A key experiential finding is that it is important to go through the entire process with a minimal amount of data to determine if in fact the approach is correct. When designing and creating the

PCPEDD process there are a myriad of decisions to be made about what algorithms to use, what features of the data are important, how to clean the data, and so on. We have found that executing the PCPEDD process multiple times with increasing amounts of data that is pristine first will help to optimize the final results.

The PCPEDD process has a timescale that is dictated by the context within which it executes (Figure 2.2). For high-frequency trading (HFT) systems, PCPEDD is executed once every few hundred microseconds. Driverless cars execute the process once every few hundredths of a second. Medical diagnosis in the emergency room is done from seconds to minutes to perhaps an hour before action on the patient is taken. On the long end is supply chain planning which can take days in the case of Amazon to years for the food supply chain or infrastructure development.

2. Planning

This phase has two faces to it. The first is strategic planning and the second is tactical planning. There are many ways to do this planning. To simplify the discussion, we choose a basic approach. A simple way to view this is that strategic planning involves defining those strategic objectives of an entity (company, NGO, or a governmental organization). Strategic objectives are those two or three things an entity must do to remain a growing concern. The difficult part is to decompose those objectives into increasingly granular activities that when executed result in the strategic objective being met or exceeded. This is tactical planning, namely, what IT, process redesign, and customer retention programs must be undertaken that when completed result in one or more strategic objectives being met.

Figure 2.3 shows this decomposition for a fictitious retail company. The strategic objective is to increase net revenues by 10% YOY. This could be one of a few. The next level down is what business programs have to be in place to ensure the strategic objective is achieved. This retailer has chosen four major business change programs which are either new or modifications of existing efforts. They have decided to increase the number of their retail locations, derive

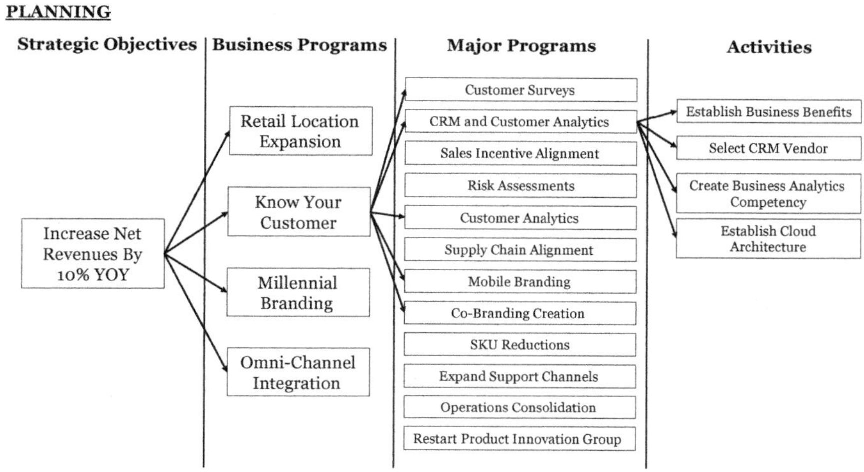

PLANNING

Strategic Objectives	Business Programs	Major Programs	Activities

Customer Surveys

Retail Location Expansion

CRM and Customer Analytics

Establish Business Benefits

Sales Incentive Alignment

Select CRM Vendor

Risk Assessments

Know Your Customer

Customer Analytics

Create Business Analytics Competency

Increase Net Revenues By 10% YOY

Supply Chain Alignment

Establish Cloud Architecture

Millennial Branding

Mobile Branding

Co-Branding Creation

SKU Reductions

Omni-Channel Integration

Expand Support Channels

Operations Consolidation

Restart Product Innovation Group

Figure 2.3: A planning process.

significant knowledge of who their customers are, either new or existing, create new branding targeting Millennials, and enable sales to be done seamlessly across channels. Each one of these business change programs can spawn one or more major programs that must be executed in order for the specific change program to be implemented. For Know Your Customer, more and effective Customer Surveys are needed, a CRM process and tool need to be implemented, a Customer Analytics set of metrics must be defined that can be used across the company, a new Mobile Branding effort must be started, and a Co-Branding partner needs to be identified and a partnership created. For the CRM and Customer Analytics major program, the Business Benefits must be established, a CRM vendor must be chosen and implementation plan completed, data scientists with experience in cross-channel and unstructured data analytics must be hired, and the current move to the Cloud the company is doing must be modified to incorporate the CRM and other enabling technologies into it.

Planning can be viewed as defining the problems to be solved and the process to solve them. Creating the chart in Figure 2.3 is straightforward enough for a team of humans with the business experience and insights into what would work for most customers of the company. Could an autonomous system do this instead? It is difficult to envision how an autonomous system could be created that when given the goal of "define a strategic objective for the company and all of the activities that would need to be done to achieve that objective," would create Figure 2.3. What rules would it execute to arrive at the Strategic Objective? How would it know that a 10% increase is an optimal number? How would a neural network be trained so that when given this information would output the need for Millennial Branding? What data would allow the autonomous system to converge to a solution that requires two Customer Analytics efforts, one within a CRM effort and one exterior to it? We know of no system to date that could even do this simple diagram on its own with no human involvement.

The negative conclusion above ends with "no human involvement." What about a human–autonomous system partnership? One can imagine the CEO and a small team interacting with an autonomous system in a manner seen with Apple's Siri. The humans would continually ask questions of the autonomous system to provide data and analytics that accelerates their thinking and instead of spending 3 months to agree on Figure 2.3, they could do it at a 2-day offsite. The autonomous system would need to have some significant rule-base associated with the company in order to execute commands relevant in the context of the company. It could fetch data from many sources across the Internet on the outcomes of various Millennial Branding efforts and summarize those results for the team. It could do a rapid assessment of where competitors are expanding or locations they were closing operations, so this company knows not to repeat those mistakes. The autonomous system could do a rapid cluster analysis leveraging public and subscription databases to determine more optimal locations for retail stores based on any number of features. At the end of the planning process, the team would know what activities to execute and also what data would need to be collected, processed, exploited, and disseminated to stakeholders for them to make decisions. The autonomous system could also create the baseline for how the data required is collected and processed. The autonomous system can provide options on data sources including what new and existing IoTs can be leveraged. It could provide the team with examples of the kinds of analytics that would be disseminated to stakeholders to ensure that what is wanted by the stakeholders can actually be used to make decisions. The key value here for the team from the autonomous system is that it can facilitate a rapid convergence to a strategic and tactical plan as well as demonstrate initial results with existing data to validate the overall approach. Efforts like this, done only by humans, take months to years. A human–autonomous system partnership should accelerate the creation and validation of the overall plan.

3. Collection

The Collection Phase is a phase that lends itself well to autonomous systems and management by an autonomous system. The collection of data can dominate the life of data scientists and others tasked with providing the analytics for stakeholders. This phase and the Processing Phase can be up to 90% of the PCPEDD process time whether that time is a few hundred microseconds or 5 years. This phase is increasingly dominated by the Internet of Things (IoT) that produce structured and unstructured data. Unstructured data constitutes over 80% of the data generated today and that number is expected to slowly grow with time. Unstructured data includes corporate e-mails, financial filings, customer feedback, blogs, online reviews, instant messages, tweets, pictures, videos, and graphs, among others. The problem with unstructured data is that the recipient of the data rarely controls the data acquisition process. A company wanting to use data from social media sites as input to sentiment analysis has zero control of the content it receives and must undertake careful collection processes and structured processing to extract valuable information from the content.

It can take years to build up the internal competencies needed to collect the right data over time and understand how to evolve that process. Collection of structured data is far easier because this type of data comes from vended sensors with well-defined APIs and data quality that must meet contractual agreements.

How well can an autonomous system perform the Collection Phase? It turns out rather well as long as the collection policies are well defined and change in a managed way. Current autonomous system systems can have thousands of sensors, whether physical sensors like cameras or virtual sensors whose input is from online sources. The Collection activities that are rote can be managed by an autonomous system. The autonomous system can use results from the PCPEDD process to adjust the type of data that is being acquired, the rate at which the data is acquired and make changes to the processing and exploitation processes if the autonomous system detects changes occurring in its domain. For example, air defense systems are completely autonomous because as they scan for incoming threats, the defense system can rapidly change its collection processes to acquire more information from other battlespace sensors if it detects a potential threat that it then confirms is real. All this might take place on timescales that humans find impossible to execute decisions. As the threat is viewed as real, the human gives permission to fire on the threat as necessary or the human can a priori indicate the system can decide on its own to fire. The key is that the system can adjust its collection processes many times on very short timescales to optimize the data it is receiving about the threat.

4. Processing

The Processing Phase is another phase that lends itself well to autonomous systems and management by an autonomous system. The Planning Phase determines that when data is collected, the processing of all data should adhere to a set of pre-determined rules; it is the process that turns raw data into actionable information.[3] Data preparation or data cleansing is a tedious process that consumes most of the time associated with PCPEDD. Estimates are about 60–90% of the PCPEDD process is the Processing Phase. There are two basic steps in the Processing Phase: cleansing and enrichment.

Cleansing data means to transform the data into new data that has problems removed and are in a format and value range to allow further processing to be done by an autonomous system. This sounds easy but in practice it is difficult and arbitrary though necessary for the correct decisions to be made. The latter process assumes that the information used is correct and optimal. The first set of corrections made to the data then is to deal with bad data. What is bad data? It is data with any number of origins: the fat thumb problem if the data is entered manually, unusual values arising from transmission errors, incorrectly formatted data, or damage to an IoT sensor that results in systematic errors being transmitted. There needs to be policies in place that govern how to consistently deal with bad data and either replace or exclude it according to well-defined criteria. An example policy is what to do if a time/date stamp is required to be in the form hh:mm:ss.ss/mmddyyyy and data is transmitted in various other formats like ddmmyyyyhhmm, hhmmss.s:ddmmyy, yymmdd, and so on. This particular policy needs to be enforced to ensure that the algorithms process the data properly. Units are another example of problems to be corrected. Information passed from IoTs are in certain units and they can be configured to output units in the International System of Units, United States Customary Units, or Imperial Units system. The obvious problem here is when systems are mixed, measurements of the same attribute will have different numbers associated with them if stated in different measurement systems. This happened to the Mars Climate Orbiter (MCO).[4] A subsystem on board MCO was supposed to output its data in SI Units and instead output them in United States Customary Units. A second subsystem that received the data was programmed to use the data in SI Units. This resulted in the spacecraft being off course and being too low and disintegrating due to atmospheric stresses. There must be policies in place to examine the metadata to determine units of incoming data and convert that data if necessary.

Once fully cleansed, the customer data is enriched with other data to form a more complete data set necessary for the proper Exploitation to be done. Often multiple streams of data are coming into the autonomous system and the autonomous system needs to perform one or more cleansing processes simultaneously before combining the data. Cleansed data can be combined to form new attributes or features based on the processing needs of the autonomous system. Typical transformations are to build models of the data (e.g., multiple regression, classification, clustering, ...); transform the data that has abnormal distributions or distributions with long tails to a more normal distribution; binning data that is so voluminous that it can be binned (e.g., time series data taken from one data point every millisecond to bin values whose centers are one second apart); transforming non-numeric data into dichotomous data (e.g., 0 and 1); and conversion of data to common formats (e.g., transforming all location data to a zip code value). Another popular technique is to perform Principal Component Analysis on the data to create new attributes or features that be used going forward.

The Processing Phase is also an 80/20 phase. Typically, 80% of the Processing Phase can be managed by an autonomous system. More often there remains that 20% of the Processing Phase that has to be completed by a human due to unforeseen problems with the data or the difficulty in doing the final one or two processing steps. In short, it is difficult to articulate a set of rules to be consistently applied to the 20% of the data by the autonomous system. The goal of any Processing Phase is to automate as much of it as possible. When data is of very high quality, 100% of the automation is achievable. This occurs, for example, in the world of HFT where the data is well-defined data coming from authoritative sources. HFTs benefit from the fact that the data and collection processes never change. The HFT autonomous system can use the incoming data to determine new course of trading options to take and modify its underlying model to reflect a new course. Most of the training of the autonomous system in this phase will be around how to deal with the 20% of the unexpected problems. Therefore, it should be expected that learning ways of dealing with this 20% will involve human–autonomous system partnerships as the autonomous system slowly learns.

At this point about 80% of the work has been done to generate actionable information. Much of the time spent is to find, collect, and process data so that it is pristine and consistent with strong data governance processes, determined empirically, put into place. Cleaning data is the most difficult and time consuming task any AS developer can undertake. Once the knowledge of how to clean data is productionalized, the rest of the fun begins.

5. Exploitation

This phase is the phase that has gotten the most attention as it encompasses the subjects of data mining and predictive modeling. Many business schools have degree programs in business analytics or data science. Those degree programs are essentially about the Exploitation Phase. The input to the phase is the data that has been prepared by the Processing Phase and its output are predictive models and other artifacts needed by stakeholders to make decisions. It is the phase that takes the most experience in doing by humans; therefore, it will take the most time to do to enable the autonomous system component of the autonomous system to function. This is the reason Google has driven so many miles with its driverless cars. Google needs to feed the autonomous system more and more data from many different situations to ensure the IoTs are producing the correct data at the correct frequency and the underlying autonomous system is learning how to operate a car in as many situations as possible.

The easiest way to think about this phase is that there are two classes of algorithms used for predictive modeling: supervised learning and unsupervised learning. Supervised learning algorithms are used when the data contains a variable called the supervisor. This variable is actually the variable that the model is going to predict. The data is integrated with the supervisor data and the model is built from this data. The model is then tested against test data where it predicts the supervisor data and compares its predictions to the actual value. The model is ready for production use when it can be shown to successfully predict the supervisor to an accuracy set by the autonomous system or human. Supervised learning is also referred to as classification where the algorithms can classify the data into known bins that are labeled by the supervisor data.

Unsupervised learning is used when the underlying data has no supervisor data. Also known as clustering, the algorithms put data into clusters that have a certain size defined by the other attributes. The user is expected to provide the label many times as it is not obvious what each cluster means and what they mean relative to one another. The output is a set of groupings or clusters of data and some meaning has to be attached to each cluster.

When the Exploitation Phase input is unstructured data, deriving meaningful models and analytics can be challenging. Extraction of insights from unstructured data is increasingly viewed as a high-valued opportunity but is still a nascent area within many companies and other organizations. Analytic techniques are increasingly important for understanding what can be learned from unstructured data sets. A key step in analyzing unstructured data is the enrichment step. Unstructured data can be used to enrich many other forms of data including structure data and it can even enrich itself, especially if it is time series data. The characteristics of the data can change with time so for an HFT, for example, it will continually monitor price data and look at new reports, CNBC videos, and recordings of earnings phone discussions to model and predict future price movement.

Can autonomous system invent new ways to mine data and produce exceptionally powerful predictive and even prescriptive models on the timescales associated with a particular autonomous system? Certainly AIs exist that are constantly optimizing the models they produce based on feedback from other autonomous system systems and from humans. The answer is "Yes" if the autonomous system has been trained already and is operating in a business context at the natural autonomous system timescales. The answer is "No" if it is not. A simple example would suffice here. Google is training its autonomous system or driverless car to operate on the streets of Mountain View, CA. The autonomous system drives all the streets in many conditions in order to learn what to do when faced with normal traffic patterns and dangerous situations. It has even encountered a woman in the road, in a wheelchair, chasing a duck with a broomstick. However, how well do the autonomous systems know that if a ball comes from behind a parked car that almost certainly a child will follow? What will it do if it stops for that child but hits black ice and begins to skid? Then what would it do? Black ice is unknown in Mountain View but it is pretty common in the Chicagoland area. How effective is the autonomous system in the Google autonomous system in driving in Chicago? It will not know how to drive in snow, hail, and thunderstorms. It will not know that the siren going off is the tornado siren and that it is headed in the direction of the storms that have the potential of creating a tornado. An autonomous system trained to drive in Mountain View, CA, will do a great job driving in towns like Mountain View but could cause significant hazards to its passengers and other cars when operating in areas that are not like Mountain View.

There will be some common elements to a Google autonomous system from Mountain View operating in Chicagoland. Many traffic laws are the same and the problems encountered in Chicago are similar to Mountain View. However, the autonomous system will have to spend time, hopefully far less, to train for Chicagoland to deal with its idiosyncrasies, such as really aggressive pedestrians. If past history is any guide, a Google autonomous system should have to be trained in a small number of cities around the country so as to encounter as many challenging situations as possible so the models developed during the learning sessions will be relevant when applied to many other situations where the models have not been trained.

6. Dissemination

The Dissemination Phase describes how actionable information is gotten into the hands of the relevant stakeholders. The new mode of dissemination here is autonomous system to autonomous system or M2M (M — machine). The Dissemination Phase is also where the blockchain[b] comes into play to record transactions that are between humans, various entities, and autonomous system. It is difficult to understand what entity can handle transactions that take place at

---

[b] See Chapter 5, Section 2 for an explanation of the blockchain.

milliseconds speeds amongst millions of autonomous system, entities, and humans. This is not a PayPal solution if the transactions
require the exchange of assets. For monetary transactions and most
other transactions that occur, this is a solution that is more akin to
the capital markets and HFTs than anything else. Parties to a trade
in the capital markets do not use PayPal. They are using the
blockchain.

Dissemination is not free. Disseminated information can be con-
tributed from a person, entity, or machine to another at no cost but
the sender and receiver are still paying for whatever device they are
using to do the sending and receiving. Most times, disseminated
information, regardless of the rates at which it is sent and received,
does require payment. The more traditional examples are data like
LexisNexis which provides subscribers with access to most legal
documents and public documents produced in the United States.
Market information such as price and volume are free if you want
them to be delayed 20 minutes or else someone (you or your trading
platform broker/dealer) has to pay the exchanges for real-time data.
In many companies, dissemination is sending business analytics to
dashboards on PCs, laptops, tablets, and smartphones.

M2M transactions are becoming the most prevalent of transactions, surpassing transactions involving humans and entities. As the
number of machines that take over more and more of the world of
work, the more transactions will be generated. A good example of
this is the factory floor that is completely automated. An interesting
business model is starting to develop that had its roots in aircraft
financing. Most do not realize that airlines do not own planes; planes
are owned by other entities that lease the planes to the airlines.
A similar business model exists on the factory floor where complex
machines and robots are not owned by the factory owner but by
some other entity or entities that lease the machine to the factory. The
owner of the machine may or may not be responsible for maintaining
the machine; in fact the owner might outsource the maintenance of
the machine as a service to the factory. In this way the factory does
not have to carry capital equipment on its books. The incentives to
lease are becoming more compelling as the factory machines,

especially robots that are highly configurable and therefore flexible, become more like autonomous system than analogue computers. Factories that are highly autonomous are more akin to data centers than they are to the factories of the twentieth century. Data centers need people with competencies in operating systems, cloud architectures and technologies, network technologies, systems management, ITIL, and operations management. The robots in factories are becoming servers with actuators. The technicians needed to service it are more like cloud architects than repair men with toolboxes.

How are the machines in the factory paid for? For completely autonomous operations, the use of a particular machine depends on the volume it produces which can be modulated based on instructions from other autonomous system in the factory or by humans. Each time the machine creates a product it can add that transaction to its own blockchain and use that to get payment from the factory owner on timescales of seconds or minutes instead of monthly. The factory owners can have instant information of how much they are spending each minute and can modulate the use of machines over timescales of minutes to hours and manage costs at a much more granular level. Once the characteristics of the autonomous factory are known and consistent, an autonomous system can be trained to eventually take over all operations, making the factory fully autonomous. The autonomous system can communicate with each factory floor machine to instruct it how quickly to assemble the next product, what changes to make to its configuration thereby changing the product it is producing. And it can do this on timescales and at costs that are far faster than any human can execute.

7. Discovery

The Discovery Phase is where decisions are made and action taken, heretofore, by humans. A key goal for an autonomous system is to be able to make decisions and take action based on the models created from the data and context of the space within which it operates. This is a topic that is the most valuable aspect of an autonomous system, is the most difficult for an autonomous system to do, and is fraught with ethical concerns. Consider human history. Prior to the 1700s, first humans and then humans and animals did all the work. Humans made all the decisions about what to plant, what to build, how to build it, who to attack, how to attack, and how best to use its only weapon, a human with a sword or club. Between the 1700s and now, machines were built to do one thing repetitively; computers allowed machines to do more than one thing repetitively; animals lost their jobs — we now pet them, bet on them, or eat them. And still humans made all the decisions. An Autonomous Revolution can be defined to be one where an autonomous system does all the work and makes all the decisions. And Humans? The autonomous system is doing the work for humans and eventually for themselves and other autonomous system machines and not Humans. If autonomous system does the work for the humans then what are the humans doing? If the autonomous system does the work for itself and other AIs, is the human life form sustainable or will the AIs pet us, bet on us, and eat us?

The scope of activities that ASs make decisions on is limited for now. Certain business processes are automated and performed by autonomous system such as manufacturing and some mining. Cars and aircraft have autonomous system controlling certain component operations. The scope of an autonomous system is growing and will continue to grow. The evolution of the driverless car, drones, and the significant parts of commercial flights that are done by the plane only. Eventually, an autonomous system will manage the entire major business process like the Insurance Claims process, manage the $100B+ portfolio of a life insurance company, manage a manufacturer supply chain from mining to finished product or at least subassembly, operate a farm, operate a slaughterhouse, operate a logistic services, and adjudicate a complex law case. The trajectory a process takes from human decision-making to autonomous system decision-making will differ for different processes. It should be expected that processes like claims management and portfolio management will become automated earlier than supply chain operations. The latter consists of many sub-processes that can be very granular and disconnected. The automation of the entire supply chain looks to occur from the bottom to top. As each sub-process is automated, it will be necessary to integrate them so they can act in an automated manner together. This integration has proven difficult in the past, but not necessarily for technological reasons but for political and policy reasons. Integration points like logistic services or loss of jobs might delay the onset of automated processes as humans fight this onset. Integration points can be used as leverage to force certain behaviors that delay the onset of automation.

The increased use of automated decisioning can also lead to ethical concerns that are only now being researched. The most evolved thinking in the ethics of autonomous system is on the use of automated decisioning for autonomous system weapons.[c] The fear is of an autonomous system arms race where not only major powers but smaller countries and terrorist organizations all now participate. The bar for nuclear weapons is extremely high while the bar for drones carrying weapons is low. The ubiquity of autonomous system weapons on a scale equivalent to that of easy to obtain weapons like grenade launchers and automatic rifles provide many more tactical uses for these autonomous system weapons. The difficulty in controlling the use of automatic rifles provides proof that controlling tactical autonomous system weapons will be as equally difficult for authorities. One can imagine a warlord providing his soldiers with rifles, ammunition, and many drones to launch to remotely attack their adversaries.

There are autonomous system weapons whose use of automated decisioning with no human intervention has been found to be acceptable. These are weapons whose sole function is defensive in nature such as an air defense system. The problem is when humans are removed from the decision loop for offensive operations. Can offensive weapons be banned from use? A counterargument to arguments for the ban is that basically the genie is out of the bottle and autonomous system weapons in the battlespace is inevitable.[5] A killer drone with a drone bought at Best Buy and an explosive payload built from

---

[c] Autonomous weapons: An open letter from AI & robotics researchers (28 July 2015), http://futureoflife.org/open-letter-autonomous-weapons/

easy-to-obtain materials can be flown to a set of GPS coordinates and explode. Autonomous system suicide bombers can be built, and built by almost anyone who can make an explosive. This argument of what to do with offensive autonomous system weapons will continue for years and consensus will be difficult as the countries with major efforts in autonomous system-based weapons will resist constraints being imposed on them.

The ability of autonomous system to make effective decisions will also adversely impact more and more jobs that are more white collar than blue collar. The growth in the breadth and depth of autonomous system decision making will slowly make more and more white collar workers redundant. People worry about the loss due to autonomous system of factory jobs and jobs typically filled by workers with at most a high school education. Autonomous system will slowly begin to replace people with college and postgraduate degrees. In short, any job that can be largely defined as a set of rules is subject to being done by an autonomous system.

But does this mean that a massive loss of jobs of up to 40% is in the offing?[6] Not all jobs can be defined by a set of rules, i.e., the decisions a human in a job has to make can be codified in a set of rules. Jobs that require artistic talents, innovation talents, and in general a talent for creative development will find the threat of autonomous system to be of little concerns. Autonomous system will continue to improve and will get so impressively fast that they will simulate non-rule based activities where in reality, the autonomous system is not self-aware or demonstrating intentionality. It just works so quickly and can learn quickly that it gives the appearance of artificial general intelligence or artificial superintelligence. This false identity could result in a significant government regulatory response that, if history is any guide, will make things worse.

With history as a guide, it is clear that every major technological and industrial change caused jobs to be lost and new jobs to be created. When the PC revolution began, no one knew that in 30 years, jobs like mobile application developer or data scientist would be needed. Not even the more prescient thinker could have imagined an iPhone more powerful than the supercomputers of the 1980s or broadband wireless connectivity or traders sitting at home with trading platforms heretofore available at Goldman Sachs. That should be the same dynamic here especially with more human–autonomous system partnerships being possible in the future.

8. The Data Gap

Does all the data needed by autonomous system systems exist? In other words, if necessary, can we collect all the data needed to support business operations? To understand this, consider Figure 1.1 above which shows the types of data and what they can be used for at different timescales. AS that operate at different time-scales need data relevant at those timescales to train the data. It shows the classes of data needed to support various business processes. The data that is least populated is data that has relevancy for months to years. An obvious example of this data would be accurate weather forecasts 6 months out. Not that this data is going to be available any time soon. However, it is possible to observe the onset of droughts through monitoring of large geographical areas. Typically, this is done with satellite imagery. However, if farms are outfitted with drones that are monitoring the growing patterns and weather conditions at farm level, large-scale maps showing the weather conditions and the onset of drought conditions should begin to show up as the data is combined on a daily basis. The data is relevant for a long period of time and not just for a point in time. Another example of this big data gap is visibility into supply chain operations that do not exist now but could exist if autonomous system systems were supporting the major processes. Again, food supply serves as a good example. It is possible with autonomous farm operations to know exactly how many cattle are alive at any one point in time, what kind of cattle they are (how old), and how those numbers change on a daily basis. Producers, who would do anything to maintain their margins, will continually whipsaw farmers to get cattle at low prices while slowing their blade speed to create an artificial supply problem for demand. Retailers such as grocery store chains typically have to pay the higher prices for meat because the whole-sale prices are artificially inflated by producers. A solution here is a more automated processing facility where farmers and retailers can match supply and demand. How relevant would producers be if automated trucks or trones (see Sec 7.2 below) brought cattle to an automated plant whose production was governed by input from the retailers? This would ensure more consistent margins for the farmers and more pricing predictability and power for retailers.

References

1. Codd, EF (1970). A relational model of data for large shared data banks. Communications of the ACM. *Classics,* 13(6), 377–387.
2. Walker, R (2015). *From Big Data to Big Profits*. Oxford: Oxford University Press.
3. Abbott, D (2014). *Applied Predictive Analytics*. New Jersey: John Wiley & Sons.
4. Stephenson, AG, LS LaPiana, DR Mulville, *et al.* (10 November 1999). *Mars Climate Orbiter Mishap Investigation Board Phase I Report*. NASA.
5. Ackerman, E (29 July2015). We should not ban 'Killer Robots,' and here's why. *IEEE Spectrum*. http://spectrum.ieee.org/automaton/robotics/artificial-intelligence/we-should-not-ban-killer-robots.
6. Frey, CB and MA Osborne (2013). *The Future Of Employment: How Susceptible Are Jobs To Computerisation?*. Oxford: Oxford Martin School.

CHAPTER 3

The Internet of Things

1. Overview

The Internet of Things (IoT) are sensors, i.e., a device that collects data and can share that data with other devices. That definition means many things to many people. This is because people see IoTs in different settings.[a] To the consumer, an IoT is a connected product like a thermostat or alarm system. In the home, IoTs can manage energy far more efficiently than today because it can manage it at a much more granular level within a home or apartment. Businesses set up IoTs with point of sales channels (e.g., at a traditional desk or else the customer can buy items as they walk along the store by scanning the bar code and using PayPal), video to track customers, real-time promotions to mobile devices depending on the information the business has about a customer who just walked in, and optimizing inventory based on what is being bought and at what pace. IoTs have matured in the manufacturing environment over the past few decades. Real-time production dashboards, health and safety concerns, and automatic quality control are just a few areas that have improved with the advent of basic sensors to address problems in

---

[a]McKinsey (June 2015) The Internet of Things: Mapping the value beyond the hype, http://www.mckinsey.com/business-functions/business-technology/our-insights/the-internet-of-things-the-value-of-digitizing-the-physical-world

manufacturing. Cities have slowly implemented IoTs to manage electrical distribution, traffic control, water management, public transportation, crime monitoring, and environmental quality. A simple and very popular IoT is used by the Chicago Transit Authority that uses GPS devices to report bus locations on a map on a mobile device and estimate when it will arrive at a stop.

The value of a sensor is measured by its ability to collect the data and the value of that data when applied to decision-making. Fig 1.1 helps to understand if the data being captured by a given IoT is of any use. Where does the data fall on that chart? Is it for short-term, medium-term or long-term data? Can it be used for more than one time-scale? Is the data one of the key features for creating the models necessary to operate an autonomous system? An IoT whose data is routinely ignored when creating and updating models is of little use to anyone.

The strength of a single IoT is necessarily less than larger numbers of IoTs deployed for use by humans and autonomous systems to make decisions. The new IPv6 Internet registration system uses a 128 bit address so it can support 2^{138} address or about 340 trillion trillion trillion addresses (3.4×10^{38}). This means that every single thing in the world, each grain of sand, corn stalk, gallon of seawater, and stalk of wheat can have its own IP address. Why does this matter? Consider an autonomous farm. Given the rapid technology evolution and generic engineering capabilities, we can assume that a corn stalk can be enabled with an IoT that can communicate with the autonomous system that operates the farm. This IoT might be attached to each stalk (think of a drone the size of a flea that flies and attaches itself to a corn stalk while the stalk is very small). The innovation process will certainly think of many ways of doing this so the idea is that each corn stalk in a farm can be connected to the farm network. This is not many stalks as a 1000 corn farm will have about 30 million corn stalks.[b] Each stalk can initialize itself with location and condition. Over the next few months, the IoT can send back small amounts of data on size and quality. It might even be able

[b]Corn production, Iowa State University Agronomy Extension, http://www.agronext.iastate.edu/corn/corn-qna.html

to send back information on what bugs have visited the stalk and weather information. The farm autonomous system can then monitor the condition of the entire crop by aggregating the information from all the 30 million corn stalks. This information can be used to optimize irrigation, fertilization, and harvesting. It can also be aggregated with similar information from years past to better understand long-term patterns and trends.

2. Evolution in Sensors

Sensors are so useful that they are popular objects to accrete additional functionality. This is a phenomena that occurs constantly in software development and has been and will continue to occur for sensors whose data is valued by its stakeholders. This implies that IoTs need to publish out their architectures especially if they become more than just transmitters of information and instead become a technology platform.

Figure 3.1 shows a generic technology platform architecture for an IoT. The architecture consists of technology services, application services, and applications that are domain specific. Table 3.1 shows each component of the architecture.

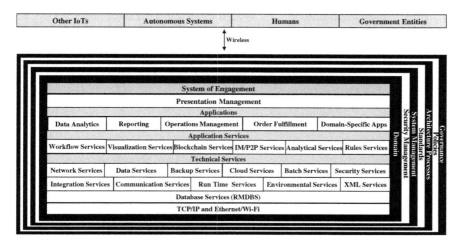

Figure 3.1:   The Technology Platform Architecture for a generic IoT.

Table 3.1: Summary of the architecture components for a generic IoT.

Area	Component	Description
System of Engagement		Manages all interactions with the external world
Presentation Management		Manages how information is displayed on all end user devices
Application	Data Analytics	Production of information to enable decision making
	Reporting	Ad-hoc reports for stakeholders based on analytics
	Operations Management	Control of processes to produce output
	Order Fulfillment	Management of paid requests by external users
	Domain-Specific Apps	Context-specific business process support
Application Services	Workflow Services	Orchestration of operations performed
	Visualization Services	Preparation of data for graphic visual representations of information
	Blockchain Services	Allows IoT to operate on a blockchain network
	IM/P2P Services	Instant messaging and peer-to-peer
	Analytical Services	Data mining and predictive analytics
	Rules Services	Management of decision logic
Technical Services	Network Services	Enables IoT to operate on any network
	Data Services	File services
	Backup Services	Secure storage of activities and data for subsequent retrieval
	Cloud Services	Enables IoT to use a cloud service for storage and compute services
	Batch Services	Execution environment for rote jobs
	Security Services	Authentication/Authorization
	Integration Services	Allows IoT to interoperate with other internal and external services

(*Continued*)

Table 3.1:   (*Continued*)

Area	Component	Description
	Communication Services	Support for various protocols
	Run Time Services	Extensions of OS services
	Environmental Services	Support for IoT operations in different software environments (dev, test, prod)
	XML Services	Support for readable file formats such as XML and JSON
Database Services		RDBMS or some other data record management
TCP/IP/ Ethernet/ Wi-Fi		Support for TCP/IP stack
Domain		Enforces the correct context on policies and procedures
Security Management		Security policies and procedures
System Management		Operational policies and procedures
Standards		Support for common standards
Architecture Processes		Architectural policies and procedures
Policies		Master to govern specific policies
Governance		Allows owner of IoT to provide enforcement of interactions and decision-making

A key attribute of IoTs is to participate in transactions. An IoT can have its own blockchain and can provide services to any other entity (human, autonomous system, or another IoT) for compensation. Why would this be important? We can consider several examples. Trading firms specializing in agriculture products are forever looking for information to give them an edge. One of the most important crop reports issued by the USDA is the May Crop Production report. It provides the first insight into how much of each crop has been planted and where. This report drives the agriculture futures markets for a long time, especially into the harvest seasons in South America, which is June, and a few months later with North American harvests. Traders do everything they can to find out what will be in that report and will use phone calls to farmers and satellite imagery to put together a trading strategy. Suppose now they could pay corn stalks to tell them what is going on in the fields across Iowa and Illinois? It is not unusual for a trader to spend $500,000 for data so if each corn stalk charges $0.10 per data point per request, a trading firm could get info from five million corn stalks about growing conditions across Iowa and Illinois. The value proposition for a farmer is that they now have an adjacent market for their crop and can increase their income, however incrementally, through selling the information generated by their crops. Or a farmer can advertise a subscription service to allow traders to download data the farmer has aggregated from the corn from the farm. It is not just traders but researchers and other consumers of this data who are interested in the provenance with the food supply chain.

A second example is in health care. Ralph Lauren now markets the PolotTechTM shirt.[c] The shirt can measure the heart rate, temperature, breathing, and balance of the wearer. The shirt communicates with the outside world via Bluetooth and an app that provides information on biometrics. This example can be extrapolated to clothes that provide as much information about the human as possible. For people over 50, a specially designed undergarment can provide continuous information on key "operational metrics" that provide proactive understanding of the onset of heart attacks, stroke, or stress-related symptoms. This data aggregated for the human can be provided to first responders and primary care physicians. The more invasive the body sensors are the more information can be provided. The human might be willing to have sensors placed in the body or bloodstream (nanorobots in the blood to

---

[c] THE POLOTECH™ SHIRT, http://www.ralphlauren.com/product/index.jsp?productId=69917696

deliver drugs — everyone's favorite example).[d] These sensors can communicate with the body sensors, which can then aggregate and store the data in situ or in the cloud. Properly anonymized, this data can be provided to hospitals and researchers to understand what they might expect in the future.

These body sensors would be useful for first responders involved in catastrophes like hurricanes and earthquakes or with military personnel deployed on the frontlines of a conflict. A soon as it is relatively safe, first responders with enter areas impacted by some weather or geological event. The sensors they wear could be outward facing to provide real time information on the situation to traditional and nontraditional stakeholders. Video of the impacted area is information-rich and provides an enormous amount of information on what infrastructure is still intact, what home and buildings are gone, damaged or relatively intact. Where is flooding, gas main ruptures, fires? These first responders wearing outward-facing sensors can provide key ground-truth information on which decisions can be made.

Traditional stakeholders would be emergency teams needing to know the extent of damage, flooding, downed power lines, and availability of infrastructure to support heavy machines and other equipment to be repurposed to help. Another traditional stakeholder would be insurance companies who can quickly begin to execute damage assessments of what is seen. Presumably, insurance companies know the locations of the homes they insure (not a good assumption in fact) and can start to inventory the damage done to policy holders. The quicker insurance companies can get claims settled and work started, the better will be their loss ratios (cost of claims paid out divided by net premiums earned). The policyholders are another stakeholder who of course want to know the conditions of their properties.

An example of a nontraditional stakeholder would be the big box retailers. The retailers that provide construction products can

---

[d]Lavars, N (17 June 2015) Nanorobots wade through blood to deliver drugs, *Gizmag.com.* http://www.gizmag.com/nanobots-blood-drug-delivery/38064/

use damage assessments to determine what materials will be needed in the impacted areas, what the best places to position the repair materials are, and how much. Presumably, the extent of the damage will render some of these stores inoperable and their inventory damaged or destroyed. The retailers can determine the extent of their losses quickly and determine how to resupply the stores with replacement materials and additional materials needed to support reconstruction. Some of these retailers have services to provide contractors to customers who have been vetted. Other big box retailers provide food and other personal items lost in the event. They too can determine the extent of damage to their properties and determine what needs to be replaced and what is additive to support rebuilding lives.

The data to augment the data from first responders can be provided by drones, manned aircraft, and satellite imagery. First responders while wearing a sensor themselves can also launch fleets of small drones with cameras with broadband filters or hyperspectral imagery. The drones could be preprogramed with a flight path to ensure all areas are covered at least twice a day to create a damage assessment baseline. The importance of the filters cannot be underestimated. Natural and man-made damage reflect light at different wavelengths so comparing before and after imagery can be useful in damage assessments. A house might look undamaged visually but viewed in the infrared could show hot spots in the house where gas fires might be burning or other damage hidden inside walls or below ground.

Imagine a policyholder who sees that their home is still there but damaged. If they go to their insurance company web site or mobile app, they can see an initial damage assessment to their property and preliminary schedules of repair. They can see who is going to do the work, where the materials are coming from, and estimated completion dates. There are offers of housing until the work is done. They could even get discounts from the big box retailers who can provide them with help where they are staying.

All of the aforementioned capabilities to create data are considered IoTs. The sensors worn by the first responders, the cameras carried by drones, and video created are all examples of how IoTs can create analytics, i.e., data with great value and capable of being used in many different ways for many different kinds of decision-making.

A future attribute of IoTs is that very simple ones can be printed and this leads to the implication that IoTs for any need and size can be printed. Imagine being able to say "print a sensor that can be attached to a utility pole to track how intense the hurricane winds will be". All the circuitry can be printed including a Wi-Fi capability so the printed sensor can connect to deliver its information. The size of the printed IoT can be customized for where it is going to be placed and the printer can add in a layer of adhesive based on the structure to which the IoT will be attached.

A word on the reason why the IoT architecture shows the stakeholder "Government Entities." A common theme in this book is that autonomous systems make it easier for the government to monitor and regulate processes such as those found in most businesses and personal lives. The desire for the government to have access to a citizen's phone makes it reasonable to assume that IoTs will also be required to acquiesce to government requests for data. Access to IoTs will take the paradigm of Big Brother to a whole new level. Do people want the government to have access to all the health data generated by the clothes we wear as part of the process for determining how health care payments work in the future? Do we want them to have access to the insurance data about the extent of home damage to make sure work is done to code? Do businesses want the government to monitor how they respond to catastrophic events to ensure some areas of the impacted area are not favored over other areas? Will access to this IoT data allow it to govern how everything is done and control all responses? These questions will become real over time and the reason the IoT architecture in Fig. 3.1 has governance and policy layers is that it is anticipated the government will demand and get more information of data that monitor processes to allow them to audit or control these processes.

3. Digital Currencies

IoTs will drive development of digital currencies because that is the best currency for IoTs to use to buy and sell services between themselves (as part of AS) and with humans. This is because not all IoTs are created equal. The data collected by an IoT has value with different value to different consumers of the data. Some IoTs might be able to take disparate data sources and fuse them into a significant data or information set. The implications are significant. This implies the existence of a blockchain to manage these transactions at high rates of speeds. This implies an IoT might have to be part of two or more blockchains. Like many other platforms, we do not know or can predict the implications to these simple questions. In fact, the evolution will be driven by the IoTs themselves and how the associated AIs evolve.

It is probably incorrect to assume that IoTs will use BitCoin or other current cryptocurrencies. It is impossible to determine ahead of time what "currency" will mean to autonomous systems who enter into transactions with one another. ASs might use different things as currency at different times and contexts. Currency might be intelligence supply, dollars, euros, or a new model that has more value for another AS than the one that created it. The key takeaway is that ASs will enter into transactions with one another and determine what has worth at that time in that context.

4. Security Challenges

IoTs turn security into a level of risk to companies and individuals to such an extent that one can perceive that risk to be almost existential in nature for that company or person. The challenge of security is a manifold problem for those who have responsibility for the sensors, whether they are legal entities, humans, or other machines. The basic problem is this: today information is gathered on most humans and legal entities. In the future, sensors will gather orders of magnitude more information on these same humans and legal entities. This new information will be more granular and more valuable to those who wish to exploit the new information. There are now more ways to breach the security of the stakeholder and once breached there is more information available to be exploited. The more information is acquired, the more ways it can be used to disadvantage the company and individual.

A difficulty that arises is this: who owns the data? In the above example of putting a printed sensor on a utility pole, who owns that data? The person who printed the IoT? The owner of the utility pole? No one? The government? If the data is wrong and leads to bad decisions being made, who is sued? An attribute of IoTs is that ownership can be ambiguous at best. Who owns the data on a driverless car whose components are printed on 3D printers by a variety of manufacturers according to government regulations and are compromised by hackers? The problem is that the security of IoTs and therefore autonomous systems start to feel like no one can claim ownership. If that is the case then how can regulatory enforcement work? There is an acute need for legal theory to catch up to technological advances.

Setting aside the issue of who owns the data, the proliferation of IoTs will present an enormous security challenge. IoTs are not designed to be secure devices — secure storage of information and transmission is an afterthought. Examine all the architecture components shown in Fig. 3.1. Many of those services are interactive services in that they interact with other services on the IoT, with other IoTs using wireless or Bluetooth, or with any other entity that it connects with for any reason. There is no way to completely secure an aggregation of IoTs and for an autonomous system, the IoTs represent the source of the security risks. The best example of this is the current and future automobile. Current cars have autonomous capabilities and we are gradually moving to driverless cars. Every car is required to have what is called an OBD II port, which is located below the dashboard on the driver's side. It is the port that a mechanic at the dealership plugs into to look for error messages and other indicators on your car's performance. It is also the same jack that the technician at the emissions control center connects to for testing your car emission. It is the easiest place on the car to connect to your car's internal network and it is the weakest link in your car. For example, in 2010, researchers demonstrated how they were able to wirelessly hack into the command centers of a 2009 Chevy Impala through the OBD-II port. They were able to manipulate the car braking system so that the vehicle suddenly stopped or failed to function at all. Wired reported that it took General Motors 5 years to completely fix the bug and ensure that future models would not have the same vulnerabilities[e]. More recently these same researchers showed how they were able to remotely break into the electronics of car through an array of security holes. In short, as cars accrete greater and greater autonomous functionality, the greater the security risk they become. Cars currently have over 100 million lines of code operating and monitoring the car performance. The complexity of this code besides just the sheer number of lines of code will increase with time. With complexity comes security problems.

What kind of problems? Consider problems with the PC or laptop. The current rage today is ransomware where a hacker can encrypt the contents of a computer and then tell the owner that unless they pay the hacker some amount of ransom in Bitcoin within 72 hours, the hard disk will be erased and everything on the computer will be lost. A hacker can do the same with the owner of a car. The hacker can lock out the owner of the car either by not allowing the key to open the car door (or if the hacker is insidious, locking the owner in the car) or not allowing the car to start until the owner pays the hacker a ransom. The problem here is that unlike the scenario with the laptop where the user can take corrective action on their own to prevent this problem from happening in the first place, the car owner has no such recourse. The car owners have no way to protect their car and are totally dependent on the car company for software upgrades and protection. Once a hacker finds a way to insert ransomware in a car, there is nothing to stop them from doing the same to every car owner who has the same car with the same security hole(s).

A final security challenge for IoTs will be the fact they will need to use digital currencies. This need, coupled with traditionally weak security capabilities, will provide an abuse of the digital currencies with new and innovative money laundering and funding of criminal and terrorist activities. For example, IoTs can be used to mine cryptocurrencies as the behest of criminal organizations or terrorist nation-states. The IoTs of

---

[e] Car hacking, Wired Magazine portal, http://www.wired.com/tag/car-hacking/

choice will be ones with not just strong security but also transactional security.

5. Privacy and Ethical Concerns

Privacy, like security, is a manifold problem for humans and legal entities. It is an issue now with just the data available in the channels of today such as Facebook, Twitter, LinkedIn, banks, and government records. The privacy issues will become more complicated and varied as more and more sensors provide data on your very life at a very granular level. Far more data on a human and legal entity will exist than they are aware of and they will not own the vast majority of the data about them. Today a human or business who is the subject of a background check, a civil suit, or a criminal investigation has far more information available to their adversaries that the human or business does not own or control. The problem with this amount of information, especially with data generated by many IoTs, is that the ability to compromise this data is easier.

The way to mitigate potential problems with IoTs is to have all the work done by the IoT be treated as transactions that are managed by a blockchain. This is a big ask if applied to individual corn stalks or other extremely numerous IoTs.

CHAPTER 4

Artificial Intelligence

1. Are There Terminators in Our Future?

So what is a Terminator? Terminators are an AI with a mind like a human surrounded by actuators and IoTs that provide it the ability to observe its environment, orient or understand its environment and context, make decisions, and then act. This is how they were portrayed in the movies and have colored our perceptions of what is artificial intelligence. A Terminator is an example of an autonomous system whose AI component is described by the Strong AI hypothesis.[1] The strong AI hypothesis states that the AI is an actual mind like a human. Is this a useful hypothesis? At this point, not really. It makes for good entertainment and the number of movies coming out with robots and people's consciousness uploaded to the Internet also tend to provide fear where fear should not exist. It also gives employment to philosophers who use it in discussions on the mind–body problem, functionalism, free will, and so on. Consciousness is not understood and should remain so for years to come. Most researchers who specialize in AI or specialize in areas that use AI as a tool rather than the object of their research are not concerned with the Strong AI hypothesis. It is the Weak AI hypothesis that is important for discussions on autonomous system and its AI component. A Weak AI model in an autonomous system has good, bad, and ugly associated with it and gives researchers, ethicists, government, and business executives much to be excited about and much to be worried about in current days and in our future.

This book adopts the viewpoint that AI will always be about computational statistics and the models derived from improvements in model development. AI software will accrete greater capabilities and speed and that the software will always *appear to be intelligent* but will never actually be intelligent. AI will never have their own minds or common sense; they will not be self-aware (at least for a very long time). The AI component of the autonomous system discussed in this book is what is always referred to as conforming to the Weak AI hypothesis. A Weak AI model will only at its best simulate intelligence but never be intelligent in the same way that humans are intelligent. AIs will act as if they are intelligent but not have actual minds or common sense. No matter how much words and perspectives describe an AI as being self-aware and sentient, the software will simply be that, software based on computational statistics that is used to created models that can help make decision by human beings or other machines at ever-increasing speeds.

Why is this understanding important for businesses, government, and the general population (i.e., a triumvirate)? The first reason is that just as the Internet forced this triumvirate to change existing processes, implement new processes, and adopt a mindset of giving up one's privacy, it is logical to assume that the use of autonomous system will force similar levels of change to the triumvirate. The key property of the triumvirate that is being surrendered is decision-making. The AI part of the autonomous system takes in information and acts on it. The human is no longer needed in rote processes. The AI component will make the decisions because the AI model is configured to execute a set of rules which have been developed based on the underlying processes. Some AIs will modify those rules over time as more information becomes available. The AI changes the rules with this new information because, as is the case with neural networks, the AI model predictions are closer to the reality it is measuring. And as with the computer systems of today, it should be expected that the AI model will act in ways that may or may not be as intended or as ethical as expected.

Consider the following example. There is a running joke within the insurance industry that when a house burns down, the owner sometimes turns out to be quite the art connoisseur based on the claims being made for expensive art lost in the fire. The online tools make it easy to create receipts for the art. Another joke is about homeowners who have an old picket fence or some such structure that has survived for years with a previous owner but with the first minor storm experienced by the new owner, suddenly finds the fence completely destroyed, even if it was the only fence in the neighborhood to be destroyed. The human knows that fraud is occurring but can be powerless to stop the fraud. The human simply lacks the ability to follow all the threads of investigations in the art world to come to an objective decision. The art would typically be of low enough value that asking a human-based service to find out about the art work is impractical. The human also lacks any history on the fence to know that there is no way with the size, intensity, and path of the storm that the fence should have been knocked down. It is easier for the human to mark the claim as proper and allow the fraudsters to be paid off.

Suppose the human had access to an AI that does fraud investigations. The human can input the information about the art work or the fence and the AI can perform a forensic deep dive. The artwork fraud would require information to be gathered about the artist, an image of the picture itself from perhaps an image on an iPhone, and the receipt. An AI trained to do very deep searches on a subject and to modify the search terms to increase the amount of quality information it is acquiring would be able to find out much more about the artist, the painting, and possible value. The AI could begin building a blockchain of the art in the house as it does its search to build a lifecycle for the art. Who painted the art? What are other pieces they have sold and for how much? Who sold the painting to the homeowner making the claim? Where did the transaction take place? Does more than one person claim to own the art? Has the same art been used in other claims (i.e., burned up several times before)? Given all the art being claimed as lost, was it physically possible for all this art to be in the house in the first place? Once completed the AI could examine the blockchain to determine if it was possible for this art to be in the house and to be worth the cost of what is being claimed.

The AI does not make value judgments when it is doing a forensic deep dive like this. It might very well uncover information relevant for one or more criminal cases. It might uncover the fact that the title to the house is in jeopardy because the title company did not do its job when these new homeowners bought the house to begin with 2 months ago. The AI might determine that the claimant is using an assumed name that they took while in Canada 34 years ago after going there to escape an arrest warrant. It might undercover the fact that one owner of the art from 22 years ago made a similar claim. What should be the next steps for the insurance company? Does it report the possible criminal information to law enforcement? Does it ignore it all? Does it deny the claim because the insured parties never disclosed certain information on their homeowners' application? At this point, any decision about what an AI fraud service would be up to the human at the insurance company. What happens if there was no human in this loop but an AI claims service that paid the AI fraud service to do the deep dive? What would the autonomous system claims service do? We presumably would assign several goals to the autonomous system claims service and one of them would presumably be a goal like "do not break any laws and report unlawful activities". So now the AI claims service has quite a few things to do above and beyond deciding to play a claim. It has to report the person with the outstanding warrant. Or it needs to determine who committed fraud — this claim or the claim 22 years ago. It has to sue the title company. The AI might decide to do it all and hand off the information to an AI that does legal work for follow up. And as far as the claim goes, is the AI required by law to pay the claim if it cannot prove the above findings? How does the AI determine whether or not it has to pay the claim? This scenario is far less contrived than the ones that discuss AI who make paper clips and attempt to show how even simple goals can cause an AI to run amok and destroy humanity. The above scenario is realistic and begins to show how basic business goals can run into issues that companies are not competent to deal with now.

It looks increasingly likely that in our future there will be nation-states or terrorist organizations that build AI for the expressed purpose of providing for the common defense or destroying enemies. Our future will have weapons owned, but not necessarily controlled by, rogue nation-states with visions of destroying most of the human race. This is because regardless of who owns the AI, the controller of the AI will determine how the AI starts to pursue its goals. These rogues will eventually have access to autonomous killer robots in ways they could not have with nuclear weapons. A simple autonomous killer robot is a drone that can be bought at a retail store or over the Internet for $300 and outfitted with a payload like ricin, fly into a crowd in a bar or underground, and deploy its payload. A large drone of the $1000+ variety can act as a kamikaze drone and carry conventional explosives into a closed facility or crowd of soft targets.

Therefore, our answer is this: Terminators (i.e., an AI with a mind like a human surrounded by actuators and IoTs that provide it the ability to observe its environment, orient or understand its environment and context, make decisions, and then act) are not in our future. What is in our future are autonomous systems in many forms (drones, robots, driverless cars and any combination of AI, analytics, and IoTs) that are programmed to perform the tasks the owners decide. These owners could be nation-states, corporations, terrorist organizations, drug cartels, or non-governmental organizations. The AI will be programmed to intentionally pursue goals consistent with the missions of their owners. What goals they actually pursue will start to diverge over time. This divergence will force the AI owners to decide if this is a good or bad divergence. If these owners turn over control of the AI to others, then there is no guarantee that the AI will pursue the goals of the owner and then who controls the divergence from the goals of the owner and who makes the decisions to mitigate the divergences.

2. Rational Agents

There are four classes of artificial intelligence: systems that think like humans, systems that act like humans, systems that think rationally, and systems that act rationally. Systems that think like humans are disadvantaged because we do not know how humans think. How do we build these cognitive models if we do not know what we are modeling? Cognitive science is an interdisciplinary practice that brings together psychologists and computer science practitioners to work together building models of how the human mind works.

Systems that act like humans are that class of AI where the Turing Test has been used to determine if a system is indistinguishable from a human. These systems are able to process spoken and written languages; they know how to store knowledge so that this knowledge is persistent and can be retrieved for use; they can use the knowledge to orient, decide, and act; and they can loop through the Boyd Loop again and again and express their actions in natural languages. Recently, there has been agreement that to pass the Turing Test, the AI must also have vision and IoTs and actuators. In short, to make systems that act like humans is to almost create intelligent life and while we can make progress in the various components, creating an AI that is indistinguishable from a human is almost like trying to boil the entire Atlantic Ocean.

Systems that think rationally are systems that attempt to logically structure a problem and provide a solution. Stated another way, could an AI have looked at data associated with the challenges of driving including deaths, costs of infrastructure, advances in technology and other areas and conclude that a driverless car is a solution for this problem and then proceed to create the solution? There is something about a human ability to converge to these solutions rather than a more logical solution that an AI would converge to for improving on driving downsides, which would be to allow everyone to fly everywhere since flying is so much safer. Could an AI provide an insurance company with a strategy to deal with its competitors in the automobile insurance business? Could an AI define a new startup to compete with Western Union in a business that is heavily regulated? For example, online startups in the remittance space still need to obtain money transfer licenses in all 50 states. What solutions would an AI come up with the deal with surviving in a heavily regulated environment? At one point, the average number of insurance-related bills introduced into the California state legislature reached a frequency of once a day. Could an AI find out that kinds of information through analysis of LexisNexis and incorporate that into a solution as part of a business case? These questions are not meant to be answered but to show how extremely difficult it can be to create an AI that can think rationally.

The last system is the system that is adopted in this book. Systems that act rationally are called rational agents. Rational agents are AI that act to achieve the best outcome possible as defined by one or more goals with the information that the autonomous system has observed. We discuss goals and making complex decisions in the sections below. A driverless car is a good example of a rational AI. It can be trained to make decisions to achieve its overall goal of driving safely. Google and other vendors achieve this by driving the cars for up to a million miles to create the models for the driverless cars to use to make the thousands of decisions it has to make while driving. These vendors can never encounter all of the possible situations that a driverless car will need to react to in order not to harm humans. When the driverless car encounters a rare situation, it needs to take some default action. A Google driverless car encountered a woman in a wheelchair chasing a duck with a broom. Not knowing what to do the car came to a stop, its default action. There will be situations when stopping is not an option. Suppose the car is on a two-lane highway and as it comes to the top of a hill it encounters a drunk driver trying to pass a car. The driverless car cannot stop or it will be hit and possibly kill the drunk driver. It cannot swerve to the left or it will hit the other oncoming car and kill or injure its passengers. It cannot swerve to the right because they are on a bridge and would go off the bridge, plunge into the icy Mississippi below, and kill or injure the family in its car. What should the car do? This scenario will happen at in some form when driverless cars become prevalent. Who decides what the default action is? The driverless car company? The insurance companies? The government whose policies tend to have unintended consequences? A human driver, presumably a parent, would probably sacrifice themselves in their actions to protect the family. How is that behavior made part of a rational autonomous system model?

3. PCPEDD Execution

Will the AI component of an autonomous system ever be capable enough to execute the PCPEDD phases? An AI is capable of doing the Collection, Processing, and Dissemination of data very well. It is capable of some Exploitation activities and does not do the Planning or Discovery phases very well. The differences can be viewed in the following way. It is possible to put into place rote processes that can be incorporated into a model that is the AI. Rote processes occur in the Collection and Processing phases and based on how well the humans do the Planning Phase, up to 90%+ of what occurs in Collection and Processing can be incorporated into an AI for execution. The Dissemination phase can also be automated to a large extent, especially if the blockchain is in use. If the Dissemination phase is subscription only then the AI has addresses to send to the subscribers without regard to the subscriber being a human using PayPal or an AI using a virtual currency.

AI models still do not perform the Planning phase of PCPEDD very well. There are AI-based tools to support the Planning process but not own the process in that the AI model can do much of the strategic work with little or no human intervention. The challenge to any AI model to do Planning is what approach does it use to develop the business strategy which is at the core of the Planning process. There are about six strategy frameworks/tools that are in use,[a] not to mention the dozens used by various consulting firms, and none of them is necessary and sufficient to develop a granular

---

[a] Balanced Scorecard, Five Forces, Growth-Share Matrix, PEST Analysis, Strategy Maps, and SWOT.

enough set of business objectives that are guaranteed to lead to AI output that will accomplish the business objectives with little or no unintended consequences. The traditional manner to create an AI model is to train it on a significant number of data. In this case, the AI model training would be fed many uses of say the Five Forces process that led to successful outcomes. This is a difficult task because there is database that contains authenticated uses of the Five Forces model and their outcomes. The author has participated in Five Forces efforts and there is never a single way of doing it. The same can be said of other frameworks and tools. There is no way to create a rote process that can be used each and every time to create the authenticated data. Training an AI assumes that the processes being modeled are rote and that enough data exists to train the model to a certain degree of accuracy. It is not possible to assign what Five Forces models were successful because success tends to be in the eye of the beholder. The company might say the consulting company they used to do the work gave them something that failed, while the consulting company, looking at the same outcomes, would say that the success was incremental. Who to believe? If there is no authenticated way to declare success, then it is not possible to train an AI to execute a business strategy in a manner consistent with humans.

Today the Collection piece is automated largely through the sensors we have discussed already as well as other sources of information (e.g., the driving laws in all 50 states and FAA flight regulations). Many sensors have well-defined operating characteristics and APIs that enable an AI model to collect data from a given sensor if the AI model needs data from the sensor or needs the data differently (e.g., the sensor provides data once a second and now the AI requires the data once every millisecond because another sensor has indicated a bad situation might start to occur and the AI rule says that confirmation is needed). An activity that the AI model cannot do is to determine what type of Collection is needed in the first place. This activity would be needed first in the Planning phase where we have already seen that an AI is not an appropriate choice to use. Another weakness for an AI in the Collections phase is to know if the sensors are optimally placed over time. For example, suppose a smart building system (effectively an autonomous system) has temperature sensors around its building and on the roof. Next to it is built a taller building with reflective windows that over time begin to induce the temperature sensors on the roof and on one side of the building to increase relative to the other temperature sensors. Has the AI model been trained to recognize the source of the temperature increase and take action? What action would it take? As long as the Collection process remains rote (a drone flies a hyperspectral camera over the farm fields once a day) then the Collection process can be well-supported by an AI and therefore an autonomous system can be deployed.

The Processing piece is automated with the various tools on the market that have AI capabilities to use to perform basic and more sophisticated levels of processing. The input of data from IoTs can be used over time to train AI models to perform basic processing of data. For imagery data, there are a number of steps required to take a raw image to the point where distances can be measured to accuracies less than an inch on the image. These steps are well-defined and can be incorporated into an AI model to use as part of an autonomous system. The challenge is what should the AI do when the processing steps need to change because the imagery being processed has changed in some manner. Typical changes would be the use of new sensors or filters on those sensors or it could be that the AI was trained on imagery of roofs in and around Dallas, TX, and now the sensors have to be used on homes in Tucson where roofs tend to be of different sizes, orientations, and composition.

Another difficulty for an AI Processing approach is how to recognize that the data being processed is compromised in some manner. For example, countries use many ways to measure the temperatures of the oceans.[2] Thermistors and mercury thermometers are placed on ships and buoys. The ship sensors can provide temperatures on the oceans as it moves around the globe. Buoys measure temperature in their specific location as they drift. At one point a problem with the collection of ship temperature data was identified and fixed. However, the examination of metadata showed that many ships decided not to implement the new protocols for a variety of reasons resulting in data being processed incorrectly.[3] How does this knowledge become incorporated into an AI model? How would an AI model determine that there is a problem with the data? This case was fortunate in that the metadata provided the confirmation of a problem. This will not always be the case and it cannot be assumed that there is an unambiguous way to identify when there are systematic errors in the data being collected. Under some scenarios then, it is clear that human expertise can still be required for the last parts of analysis because that knowledge cannot be coded into an AI or at least evolved from the AI.

This is also true of the Exploitation phase where existing tools are able to automate the Exploitation phase but at some point, human expertise is needed earlier on in the process to finalize creation of the actionable analytics. There is a long history of the automatic creation of actionable metrics such as financial performance, customer analytics, and supply chain operations that are consumed by humans and machines alike. One of the benefits of ERP systems is that they are preloaded with many of the metrics required to operate a business and satisfy regulatory reporting requirements. The maturity of the roles of CFO and COO are such that everyone agrees on what various metrics mean and how they are calculated. Regulatory reform has enforced this uniformity. What about the analytics associated with processes that are not as mature or understood? Can an AI be trained? Do humans know enough about these processes to train the AI model?

Consider the drought in the Midwest that occurred in 2012. A drought can be considered to be a gray swan event because of the large-scale impact it could have. Table 4.1 shows the sequence of announcements made by the USDA leading up to a declaration that drought conditions existed. A good question would be how could the USDA go from optimistic to pessimistic in a 2-month period? An examination of the NOAA Palmer Hydrological Drought Index of the growing regions in each state shows that as early as January 2012 the conditions for drought were on the map

Table 4.1:   Timeline of 2012 drought announcements by the USDA.

Date	Announcement
September 30, 2011	End-of-year estimate of grain stocks is 1.13 billion bushels. This estimate is 30% lower from prior years and the lowest since 2004.
March 30, 2012	First 2012 planting estimate released by USDA. This estimate confirms analyst expectations of high acres planted.
May 10, 2012	USDA estimates that yields will be up throughout much of the Corn Belt.
July 11, 2012	USDA announces that 60% of the Corn Belt is suffering from drought and that corn quality is as poor as has been seen since 1988.
August 10, 2012	A per-acre yield of 123.4 is announced by the USDA. This yield is the lowest since 1995.

of the United States. Monthly updates of the map show how the conditions grew and persisted until the surprise USDA announcement in July 2012. Could an AI model be trained to recognize drought conditions earlier on and at least provide warnings to farmers of the upcoming drought? The answer here is yes as the onset of a drought can be defined in terms of the Palmer Index which is a moisture measurement.[b] An Index of less than −2.0 identifies a region to be in drought conditions. The first half of 2012 showed that many regions in the Midwest had drought areas and that this behavior was uncommon when compared with the Western States which seem to be in a perpetual state of drought. NOAA has this data going back decades so it is possible to define rules that an AI can be trained. Some will argue that determining a drought is very difficult as NOAA does on its web site. This should not prevent an attempt to define the drought criteria that can be applied. As shown in the chapter on autonomous farms, drought

---

[b] National Climatic Data Center (15 May 2013) Climate of 2013 — April U.S. Palmer Drought Indices. http://www.ncdc.noaa.gov/oa/climate/research/prelim/drought/palmer.html

maps of the United States can be constructed from measurements taken during the operations of a farm by the autonomous system that operates the farm. Therefore, very granular maps can be made that should provide better criteria for determining when a drought condition exits and get that warning out to farmers before the drought becomes a problem.

Another way of asking the question (will the AI component of an autonomous system ever be capable enough to execute the PCPEDD phases) is can autonomous systems cope with black swan and gray swan events? For the purposes of this book, we define a black swan event to be an event where it is very hard or impossible to assign a realistic probability of occurrence to it. This would include the rise of the Internet and the PC. We define a gray swan event to be one where a good or reasonable probability of occurrence can be determined and used. Example of gray swans would be an airplane crash whose probability of occurrence is well known. When autonomous systems encounter a gray swan event, will they be capable of dealing with it? Will the Planning phase be of sufficient rigor that all gray swan events at least will be reflected in the goals of an autonomous system?

4. Goals and Making Complex Decisions

AI are present in rote business processes and their use are slowly expanding. The AI competency tends to be embedded across organizational competencies with expertise in specific software or hardware but not in the overall understanding of what an AI does. This should change as the use of AI expands. Companies should expect their organizations to create new roles in a manner similar to how IT competencies evolved with time in companies from the mid-1980s until now. One of the long-term problems that existed and still does is this: Is a company a technology-driven company or a business-driven company? What is meant by this is does the company develop its strategy by letting the technologies (new and existing) lead and ask business units to conform or does the company develop its strategy as a business-led effort and then develop a technology strategy to support it? Or does a company do both (unfortunately too common) where business pursues its own technology agenda and technology chooses systems that box business processes in? The same dynamic will arise for AI. Will the company implement AI to support its operations from the technology side or from the business side?

The stakes here are much higher than just picking a wrong technology vendor or in picking one of every flavor. The AI component is not just software that is built once and runs. It is software that changes with time. The data that it processes to do its job will be used to continually improve the underlying AI models and over time these models will hopefully get better and better. The more breadth and depth the AI models have to support the business processes, the more critical they are to the business. The more critical they are to the business and their model optimized, the less the business would want changes. What does a business do if it discovers that the AI model is pursuing goals in a manner inconsistent with the business? And that it has been pursuing the wrong goals for a long time? It is no longer a question of changing the configuration of the software to undo the rules that are causing the problem. In principle, the AI would have to be retrained on years worth of data with no guarantees that the AI models that came from the corrective effort are any better than the models that exhibited undesirable behaviors.

How is it possible to know if the goals given to an AI that supports business processes are the correct goals and will not result in unintended consequences occurring? In the movie *Fantasia*, Mickey Mouse is the sorcerer's apprentice. As the sorcerer is performing magic, Mickey has to cart water from a well to a cauldron. After the sorcerer leaves, Mickey decides to use the sorcerer's hat to enchant a broom to carry the water for him. Mickey then falls asleep as the broom does what it was told to do, namely, carry water from the well to the cauldron. When Mickey awakes he finds that the broom is still carrying the water from the well to the cauldron but that the room is now flooded because the cauldron is overflowing. The broom had only one goal but it did not have a goal to not flood the room or cause damage. This is called the Sorcerer's Apprentice Problem or "perverse instantiation."[c4] Basically, the goals of an autonomous system, being representative of the goals of the designer, might be coded and tested in the program but there is no guarantee that the autonomous system will actually act as intended by the designer.

Figure 2.2 shows that autonomous system can be viewed as continually executing the PCPEDD loop. The HFTs are now mature autonomous trading systems that should eventually not require human help to achieve their goals and in large part do that now. Defensive military systems have limited autonomy in functions such as bomb disposal, mine clearance, and anti-missile systems.[5] How complex does a situation have to be for a completely autonomous solution that collects data, processes it, and makes decisions to become a threat or at least identified as an amoral or illegal activity from the perspective of humanity? As our world transitions to more and more autonomous capabilities becoming key parts of our lives (e.g., new autonomous braking systems on cars), will we be able to cope with the problems that will be encountered as new and immature systems work to refine their goals based on constant use and testing?

Autopilots have been used on aircraft for years and have a great safety record. This has caused them to accrete more and more functions with time. At present, an autopilot can almost govern the whole flight process though the process is actually engaged into the flight, disengaged within a certain distance of the destination, and disengages if the situation requires the use of a human being. Air France Flight 447 crashed on June 1, 2009.[d] The aircraft pilot tubes were obstructed by ice crystals and caused the autopilot to disengage. The report synopsis lists the events that lead to the crash and the events are dominated by errors made by the flight crew after the autopilot disengaged. Here is an example of what can be expected as

[c] Soares, N (2015). The value learning problem., Machine Intelligence Research Institute. https://intelligence.org/files/ValueLearningProblem.pdf

[d] Final report on the accident on 1st June 2009 to the Airbus A330-203 registered F-GZCP operated by Air France flight AF 447 Rio de Janeiro — Paris. BEA. 5 July 2012. https://www.bea.aero/docspa/2009/f-cp090601.en/pdf/f-cp090601.en.pdf

more autonomous systems control business processes yet cannot cope with gray or black swan events and the humans, having lost their expertise through allowing the autonomous system to do all the work, also now do not have the expertise to resolve the problem.

This is an example scenario where the combination of a human and autonomous systems should have a valuable impact. Autonomous systems that support longer terms processes such as those in various supply chains are almost non-existent except for very tactical solutions that operate within well-defined limits. Companies need to specify the goals of their supply chain elements to such a degree of certainty that they will not have multiple perverse instantiations throughout the supply chain operations, especially when black and gray swan events occur. At this point and far into the future, governance over complex processes like a supply chain will increasingly be done by a human and autonomous system or systems. This combination has the ability to execute the Observe-Orient-Decide-Act phase faster than a black swan event or a gray swan event. The combination offers up the possibility of a positive use of humans and autonomous systems. The human has an opportunity to see the onset of a gray swan event such as a drought or plane that is out of control and take corrective action. Everything the human needs to make a decision is provided by the autonomous system including possible courses of action. The action might not be to stop the gray swan event, as in the case of a drought, but to use other mechanisms to mitigate the impact of the event. This also, we believe, provides insight into how those humans that lose their jobs due to automation might find new jobs. They need to find ways they can partner with an autonomous system to provide value to others.

5. Bounded Vs. Unbounded

Dr. Henry Kissinger published an article detailing his belief that artificial intelligence (AI) is a problem, probably an existential problem.[6] Dr. Kissinger joins Elon Musk, Bill Gates, Stephen Hawking, and others who have come out to declare AI is an existential threat. He should be commended for doing this. His views are influential to a wider audience, many of whom are leaders in non-technology areas. Dr. Kissinger's newfound interest in ethical AI should attract the attention and interest of those leaders as well. However, he commits the same error that many people do when concluding that AI is an existential threat: the conflation error.

The conflation error comes about when the success of AI programs such as chess and Go are conflated with similar successes that could be achieved with AI programs when they are used in supply chain management or claims adjustments. This is called the bounded vs. unbounded problem. The rules of games like chess and Go are well bounded. The rules are prescriptive, somewhat complicated, and never change. A book teaching chess or Go written 100 years ago is still relevant today. Training an AI to play chess or Go takes advantage of this boundedness in a variety of interesting ways including letting the AI decide how it will play.

Now imagine that the rules of chess can change randomly at any time in any location. Chess on Tuesdays in Chicago has one set of rules but in Moscow, there are a different set of rules on Thursdays. Chess players in Mexico use a completely different board, one for each month of the year. In Sweden, the roles each piece takes can be decided by a player even after the game starts. Suddenly it becomes impossible to write down the rules that everyone can follow at all times at all locations. This is an example of an unbounded problem.

AI is today being applied to business systems like claims and supply chains who, by their very nature, are unbounded. It is impossible to write down all the rules that an AI has to follow when adjudicating an insurance claim or managing the supply chain for something as simple as bubble gum. The only way to train an AI to manage one of these is to feed it massive amounts of data on all the myriad processes and companies that make up an insurance claim or a simple supply chain. We then hope that enough data has been used to produce a model that not only does the job but does it ethically. It is impossible to know ahead of time if these conditions are met. It can take a year or more to ascertain this. In addition, changes in the form of new regulations, changing market demand, and new technologies ensure that rules associated with business systems are continually changing thus keeping these systems unbounded.

Therefore, the argument that conclusions about the capabilities of AI based on bounded systems can be applied to unbounded systems is never true. Humans are excellent when applying AI to bounded systems and weak, at best, when applying AI to unbounded systems. We are just learning how to incorporate AI models into parts of unbounded systems. We have managed to create AI loan systems that are biased against certain segments of our population while at the same time creating self-driving cars that are far better than most human drivers. We are only beginning to understand how AIs applied to unbounded systems make their decisions as it is very difficult to interrogate the AI and ask why a particular decision was made. The recent fatal accident in Tempe, Arizona in which a self-driving car was involved demonstrates this vividly. The authorities had to rely on many sources of information, including the car itself, to determine what actually happened. The car provided telemetry back about it operations but was incapable of answering the question "why did you hit the pedestrian?"

This lack of precision in how we describe the use of AI is giving rise to a significant apprehension on its use in self-driving cars, automated farms, drone airplanes, and many other areas that would benefit from a substantial use of AI. Most people are not willing to get into a self-driving car based on recent surveys. They are afraid that the AI will put them in greater danger than a human. This concern can in part be traced directly back to the *Terminator* and other science fiction movies that position AIs as evil and endow them with unrealistic capabilities. It can be traced back to how companies are trying to field self-driving cars without first demonstrating the benefits of these cars. And it can be traced back to well-known and well-meaning people making pronouncements about existential threats when, in fact, none exist and there is no proof yet that they can exist. Research does need to continue in this area. However, worrying about Terminators is like worrying about overpopulation on Mars given all the talk of missions to the Moon and to Mars. Who knows if it will happen?

References

1. Stuart, R and P Norvig (2009). *Artificial Intelligence — A Modern Approach*. 3rd Ed. New Jersey: Prentice Hall.
2. Rennie, JJ *et al.* (2014). The international surface temperature initiative global land surface databank: Monthly temperature data release description and methods. *Geoscience Data Journal*, 1, 75–102.
3. Kennedy, JJ et al. (2011). Reassessing biases and other uncertainties in sea surface temperature observations measured in situ since 1850: 2. Biases and homogenization. *Journal of Geophysical Research Atmospheres*, 116 (D14), D14104.
4. Bostrom, N (2014). *Superintelligence*. New York: Oxford University Press.
5. Thornhill, J (25 April 2016). Military killer robots create a moral dilemma, FT.com. http://www.ft.com/intl/cms/s/0/8deae2c2-088d-11e6-a623-b84d06a39ec2.html#axzz46r8ijFVQ.
6. Kissinger, H "How the Enlightenment Ends", *Atlantic Monthly*, June 2018.

CHAPTER 5

Autonomous Systems Enablers

1. 3D Printers or The Devil Prints Prada

Hurricane Sandy devastated the New Jersey Shore in 2012 and was the second costliest hurricane in US history at $71.4 billion of damage. This area of the East Coast suffered the most damage of all the areas impacted. Every home in the town of Mantoloking suffered damage. This town is on a narrow piece of land that separates the Atlantic Ocean from Barnegat Bay. Mantoloking has a bridge that runs from Highway 35 across the Bay to the mainland. The only other way out is Highway 35 North which is a two-lane congested road that eventually ends up on the mainland. The bridge was destroyed as were portions of Highway 35. And while citizens were evacuated, many homes just disappeared. There are stretches of land along the beach that are empty now where once stood the beach homes of many residents of the New York/New Jersey metropolitan area.

Home repairs and rebuilding has been slow. Four years after the event, many residents who lost their homes are still living in temporary housing and hotels while the State of New Jersey, the Federal Government, and many insurance companies argue over whether homes should be torn down and replaced or just repaired. Years later the streets of Mantoloking are filled with park trades vans that are working continually to fix or replace the damage.

There is no estimate of when the work will be completed and all claims resolved.

Some of the homes that were torn down are being replaced with fabricated homes. These are pre-built homes where the foundation is laid and then the house is placed right on top of the foundation. One resident interviewed for this book told of watching a house being placed on the foundation next to her and she watched as the house slowly moved in place. Inside the chandeliers gently swung back and forth. The popularity of pre-fabricated homes was something of a surprise to most residents but it does make sense if one is desperate to have a house back and a normal life to live. But why do people have to wait four years for their new home when one can be created in a matter of weeks using 3D printing? If there was a scenario where printing home materials in large quantities using waste materials recycled from a catastrophe, restoring the Jersey Shore would be that scenario.

A Chinese company has now verifiably printed homes and other large structures.[1] Winsun has built ten homes made out of recycled concrete, a six story apartment building, and a 12,000 square foot villa. The company has built a 3D printer that measures 20 feet tall, 33 feet wide, and 132 feet long. The input to the machine are CAD drawings of home components and materials blended from concrete blocks, fiberglass, sand, and their patented hardening material. The output from the printer are the components needed to build the structure. Winsun claims that the cost of the structures is 60% lower, takes 30% of the time to complete the construction, and uses 80% less labor than conventional construction methods. Components such as electrical wiring, pipes, windows, and doors were made conventionally and fitted afterwards as the printed components were made with space for these additions.

Manufacturing via 3D printing is commonly referred to as additive manufacturing because printed parts are created by adding layer upon layer of a material to build out the compete object. At this point 3D printing is done of components added to conventionally manufactured items.[2] The world is a long way away from all manufacturing being done using 3D printers. However, results at the present clearly show that this technique has begun to scale up and there is line of sight to additive manufacturing becoming the dominant mode of how products are produced. A useful example are jet nozzles. A typical jet engine has between 10–20 nozzles. Made conventionally, a nozzle requires the machining and welding of about 20 parts. This process results is labor intensive and has a non-trivial amount of waste produced. GE is now printing the fuel nozzle for jet engines, something unthinkable even a few years ago. It is producing about 25,000 nozzles annually for new jet engine production. GE does not provide exact numbers except to state that the printers run constantly producing simple to complex nozzles and without the same level of waste products. This approach allows then to manufacture a product faster and less expensively than conventional means.

3D printers could be a gray swan event for society. It offers the possibility of providing parts in hours vs. months for the US Marines whose needs are immediate and expensive.[3] Surgeons can print heart valves specifically for a person instead of trying to match the size of a replacement valve made from cow or pig hearts. New product development practices can print ideas quickly for prototyping and market testing prior to making large-scale manufacturing commitments. Old and missing parts for cars and machines can be fabricated if a drawing for it can be created. The source material for the layers (i.e., the "ink") can be just about any material from recycled concrete to living cells. Apparel such as shoes and eye frames are now being printed and sold commercially.[4] The FDA has approved the manufacture of pills using 3D printing techniques.[5] Firearms can also be printed.

The impact of 3D printing can be significant. Most extrapolations of the future where 3D printing exists conclude that the world is heading for a new enlightenment or doomed. Certainly, 3D printing, if it can meet its future performance expectations and scale, will have a significant impact but what will be the scale of that impact. Will the impact be gut-wrenching or just a new toy for hobbyists? In the chapter on Manufacturing we discuss the impact of 3D printing in the context of autonomous system. Our conclusion is more gut-wrenching than new toy.

2. The Blockchain

We have all played that game of "telephone" where you have a long line of people. The first person states a fact only to the person next to them. This second person then turns and states this fact to their third person. The third person does not know what the first person told the second person and must trust the second person has told them what the first person has said. On it goes to the 100th person who hears from the 99th person. The 100th person that states out loud what the first person said. Ten times out of ten, there is little agreement between the first person and the 100th person. The information has been corrupted through its retelling even if no one attempted to corrupt the message. Now consider if someone really did want to compromise the delivery of the message of the first person. It would be quite easy for them to perturb, even slightly, the message knowing full well that the rest of the line will continue with slight to moderate modifications over time. The blockchain guarantees that what the first person says is transmitted exactly as is to the 100th person with no changes imposed and inserted by malfeasant behavior.

Never heard of the blockchain? You should because it is the technology that will very well underpin the transformations occurring in many industrial sectors and allow for M2M transactions that are part of those transformations. The blockchain over time could very well be a black swan event that has as much impact to our society as the Internet. The Internet matured over many years until 1995 when the last restrictions on use of the Internet that limited commercial traffic were removed.[6] Within 10 years it became a dominant infrastructure for the business world. Business models went from having largely manual mission-critical processes to those processes being managed by applications running on the Internet. Today, business models assume the existence of Internet services as much as they assume the existence of electricity. By 1995 the World Wide Web was in use but unknown to the commercial sector. Today business models have not only incorporated its technologies into it mission-critical processes, they have also embraced the use of similar technologies that support mobile (i.e., remote) operations. It is reasonable to assume that the blockchain will, in time, mature from its current state to something far more mature and sophisticated. New features as fundamental as the World Wide Web can be expected to be developed for the blockchain that will make its presence as important as the Internet and electricity.

The manner in which the blockchain will effect this transformation will probably be as pervasive and stealthy as the double-entry bookkeeping was when it was introduced in 1494. Accounting as we know it today got its start in Genoa, Italy, from Franciscan friar Luca Pacioli who also wrote the first book on accounting. It became another tool and its use quickly spread but in not so explicit a manner. Soon no company in Europe and eventually the New World could operate without double-entry bookkeeping. It supported the massive changes seen in the First and Second Industrial Revolutions. And it is still in use today supporting the gut-wrenching changes we have seen recently. Some have argued that double-entry bookkeeping was part of the oxygen that allowed capitalism to flourish (insurance being the other).

What is it about the blockchain that makes it a potential black swan? The disruptive attribute of the blockchain is that it removes the need of trusted third parties. What are trusted third parties? These are entities that the parties in a transaction trust to validate that the transaction is executed according to existing law. What are these entities? Many things are in fact. Banks, investment firms, governments, accountants, and even currencies are all trusted third parties.

Is it realistic to expect existing trusted third parties to disappear due to something as straightforward as a blockchain? The history of new technologies is replete with examples of them never living up to their initial expectations. It is reasonable to assume that the same will happen with the blockchain. Issues with scaling the blockchain to support the trillions of daily transactions that occur each day is one major issue. The second is that existing trusted third parties will do all they can to maintain their dominant positions and control the evolution of the blockchain so as to make this evolution work to their advantage. AT&T, Comcast, Facebook, Google, Apple, and others have been successful in becoming the Internet for the world as far as the world is concerned. The world does not use the Internet directly; they use apps on their phones, tablets, laptops, TVs, and PCs controlled by the aforementioned companies. It should be expected that a similar dynamic will occur with the blockchain. Whoever owns the blockchain that records the transactions of some asset (homes, cars, futures contracts, diamonds, Bitcoins, ...) will come to dominate how those business models, that depend on transactions involving those assets, operate.

How does the blockchain work? Figure 5.1 shows the sequence of events for a simple transaction. The blockchain is a shared and trusted public ledger that anyone can view but no one owns or controls. "Distributed, shared, and trusted" mean that the participants

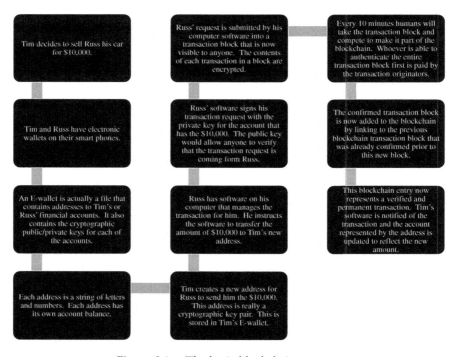

Figure 5.1:   The basic blockchain process.

in the blockchain system collectively manage the blockchain. The blockchain is structured so that changes to it occur in a controlled and rule-based manner. The blockchain ledger ensures that double-spending does not occur. Transactions are a permanent record in the blockchain.

This transaction involves the exchange of dollars but could involve instead transactions between autonomous systems, provenance of food, medical procedures, insurance claims, deeds and titles of ownership, a person's CV, or votes. We will not go into a transaction in all its details as those can be found[7] elsewhere.[a] The bottom line is that the blockchain is a way to distribute trust.[8] The blockchain allows for two entities (human or non-human) who have no prior relationship to enter into an agreement that involves the exchange of something of value (currency, information, physical asset) and ensures the transaction is consummated as expected.

How useful will the blockchain be? The answer to that question remains to be answered. The public blockchain will always be useful to cryptocurrencies so as long as they are relevant, the public blockchain will be relevant. There are two classes of blockchains: public and private. The public and private blockchain have many similarities such as decentralized peer-to-peer networks, where each participant maintains a replica of a shared append-only ledger of digitally signed transactions, how they maintain the replicas in sync through a protocol referred to as consensus, and how they provide certain guarantees on the immutability of the ledger, even when some participants are faulty or malicious. Bitcoin is a public blockchain.

The sole distinction between public and private blockchain is related to who is allowed to participate in the network, execute the consensus protocol and maintain the shared ledger. A public blockchain network is completely open and anyone can join and participate in the network. The network typically has an incentivizing mechanism to encourage more participants to join the network. A private blockchain network requires an invitation and must be validated by either the network starter or by a set of rules put in place by the network

---

[a] Bitcoin, Wiki, https://en.bitcoin.it/wiki/Main_Page

starter. Businesses who set up a private blockchain, will generally set up a permissioned network. This places restrictions on who is allowed to participate in the network, and only in certain transactions. Participants need to obtain an invitation or permission to join.

The widespread adoption of the blockchains will come from the private blockchain. Can companies find uses for the private blockchain in their domain?

Blockchains are overhyped. One reason is that people do not understand that they are a replacement for a pretty mundane thing called a database. A person must ask themselves "what is the problem they are trying to solve?" In many cases, the solution can be implemented perfectly well using a relational database such as Oracle and SQL Server. If your solution can be implemented using the latter, then do it. They have decades of maturity behind them and vast human expertise available. Blockchains have only been around for timescales measured in months, not decades.

3. The Smart Contract

A second concept that uses a blockchain is the smart contract.[9] is the original definition of a smart contract was:

> *A smart contract is a computerized transaction protocol that executes the terms of a contract. The general objectives of smart contract design are to satisfy common contractual conditions (such as payment terms, liens, confidentiality, and even enforcement), minimize exceptions both malicious and accidental, and minimize the need for trusted intermediaries. Related economic goals include lowering fraud loss, arbitration and enforcement costs, and other transaction costs.*

This was the first definition of a smart contract. Smart contracts are not contracts that we encounter in our lives and businesses. They are not better versions of legal contract that have some special capabilities that make them superior to the contracts businesses and humans sign every day. They are not the contracts that are adjudicated in a court of law.

Smart contracts can be thought of as business rules encapsulated on a private block chain. The rules are software code embedded into the block chain and are executed every time a transaction is added to a block or a block added to a block chain. Think of them as similar to database triggers. Examples of smart contracts are to determine the attributes of a transaction given the context of the transaction execution.

Smart contracts are created by developers who must work with those with the business acumen to define how the smart contract is to work. Like triggers, smart contracts take up processing time and too many contracts will slow the block chain update process down. Smart contract testing is key because of the experiences in the past with circular contract rules.

4. The TRONE

The use of driverless trucks is gaining traction in the marketplace. Trucks are mainly used as the logistic component of supply chains. Supply chains have become far more automated and rigorously scheduled in the past twenty years with the advent of lean manufacturing and emphasis on quality management. The movement of raw materials to component manufacturers to assembly plants and then to the end customer is a highly orchestrated process and trucking provides the key integration process. Trucks use the major transportation infrastructure and exert significant stress on this infrastructure. They are also involved in accidents with a total of 3,852 fatalities in 2015, approximately 10% of total vehicle fatalities.

The goal should not be to improve a truck with driverless capabilities. Trucks have greater challenges than cars when creating the AIs to operate them. There can be significant aerodynamic changes due to loads and configurations, not to mention road conditions. Ever see a truck maneuvering the streets of Chicago. It is not a pretty sight.

The goal should be to start removing trucks from the road by developing and deploying truck drones or trones that can carry loads of up to 5000 pounds to a maximum distance of 1000 miles with the goal of reaching 50,000 pounds and 2,000 miles. The business case for truck drones shows that there is significant upside and no loss of benefit to existing carriers, truck drivers, and tax receipts. The benefit to supply chains is simplifying the logistics component with trones that has positive benefits to a supply chain's agility to changing conditions such as hurricane damage, adaptability to changing demands of companies and consumers, and aligning performance of supply chain partners. A key attribute of a trone is that they can fly direct routes from the pickup point to the delivery point. There are no intersections, traffic lights, on-off ramps, and other vehicles to contend with while on their route.

It is a matter of time before trones are built to move loads of this size cross-country. This is not a research problem but an engineering problem. The size and payloads of trones is increasing with time. The two largest known at this time are the Air Mule by Urban Aeronautics and the Griff 800 by Griff Aviation (neither a U.S. company) which can carry loads over 1,000 pounds for 45 minutes and more. The Defense industry are working on trones that can easily find their way into the commercial sector.

5. Augmented and Virtual Reality

We are all familiar with augmented reality (AR). We see it all the time on the TV when we watch a sporting event. The animations on screen such as the scoreboard, the first down lines in football games, Eddie Olczyk using a telestrator to show what the Chicago Blackhawks did right or wrong on the ice, or the time differences between race cars are AR. AR are artifacts that enhance and enrich our experiences.

Virtual reality (VR) is a digital experience that replaces the real world with a virtual world. Think the Star Trek Holodeck. VR currently requires a gaming engine to create the new 3D world and a set of goggles to visualize the 3D data that is continuously updated as the human moves through the virtual world. The virtual world could be fictitious or a rendering of a real object like a car, airplane, or

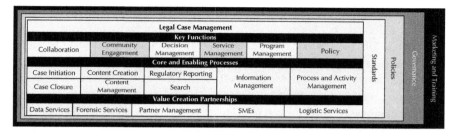

Figure 5.2:   The business model for a law practice.

construction machine. The latter are useful for training and has the added benefit of not needing the real thing to operate.

AR and VR could be used to train the AI component of an AS based on an immediate need or at least a perceived future need. Suppose an AS experienced a context where its performance was not optimal (e.g., a car in extreme weather conditions). The AS could recreate the context with many slight changes and retrain its extreme weather model to operate safer when such conditions are encountered. In essence, the car creates a virtual world similar to the one it just encountered to retrain itself. It could then offer that model up to other cars to use if the other car decides to purchase it.

References

1. Sevenson, B (18 January 2015). Shanghai-based WinSun 3D Prints 6-Story Apartment Building and an Incredible Home., 3D Print.com. https://3dprint.com/38144/3d-printed-apartment-building/
2. LaMonica, M. Additive Manufacturing GE, the world's largest manufacturer, is on the verge of using 3-D printing to make jet parts. *MIT Technology Review.* https://www.technologyreview.com/s/513716/additive-manufacturing/
3. Bacon, LM (30 April 2016). Here's how Marines are using 3-D printing to make their own parts. *Marine Corps Times.* http://www.marinecorpstimes.com/story/military/2016/04/30/heres-how-marines-using-3-d-printing-make-their-own-parts/83544142/
4. Fitzgerald, M (28 May 2014). With 3-D printing, the shoe really fits. *MIT Sloan Management Review.*

5. Palmer, E (3 August 2015). Company builds plant for 3DP pill making as it nails first FDA approval. fiercepharmamanufacturing.com
6. Harris, SR, Gerich, E (1996). Retiring the NSFNET backbone service: Chronicling the end of an era. *ConneXions* 10 (4).
7. Makamoto, S. *Bitcoin: A Peer-to-Peer Electronic Cash System.* https:// bitcoin.org/bitcoin.pdf (The original paper).
8. The promise of the blockchain: The trust machine (31 October 2015). *The Economist.* http://www.economist.com/news/leaders/21677198-technology-behind-bitcoin-could-transform-how-economy-works-trust-machine
9. Szabo, N (1994). *Smart Contracts.* http://szabo.best.vwh.net/smart. contracts.html

CHAPTER 6

The Global Food Supply

1. Introduction

Ever tried milking a cow? It can be a very challenging environment to work and the best analogy is having your office in the restroom of a very busy airport. Milking barns tend to be open at one or both ends to the outside. They have to be to vent the gases that arise from the presence of a dozen to hundreds of dairy cows. Cows do not know that a human is standing nearby trying to hook them up to a milking machine at 6 a.m. in the morning when they are flatulent, urinate and defecate. And they do not realize that their presence represents a heat source that can force a farmer to wear only a tee shirt in the dead of winter while milking them. Cows do not follow instruction but can be trained over time. Ever tried moving a 1400 pound dairy cow into a stall they do not want to go into?

Do you think cows take a day off? Cows typically have to be milked twice a day without fail or you can lose a valuable dairy cow. That means that Illinois dairy farmers have to be out milking cows at 6 a.m. and 6 p.m. Christmas morning and evening in subzero temperatures. Milking cannot stop if the farmer has the flu or a broken arm or mourning the loss of a close friend or relative. Those cows have to be milked and at 6 a.m. in the morning when a parent wakes up having to feed children on their way to school; they do not think of the farmer who allows them to reach into the refrigerator and grab a staple of their diet.

The milk truck sometimes shows up on Christmas day. Or Thanksgiving. Or when the farmer has the flu. The driver takes his load to a processing facility where the milk is pasteurized, bottled, and shipped out to local retail outlets. The total time from cow to store is about 48 h.

If dairy farming is not for you, then what about apple orchards? Contrast the farmer who has an apple orchard with the dairy farmer. Having large rows of trees that appear to be mainly low maintenance and are easy on the eyes appears to beat dairy farming anytime. No planting, no 6 a.m. Christmas mornings, no waste products, and no belligerent animals to deal with at −10°F. Once a year for about 6–8 weeks, the farmer gets to go tree to tree to fill up containers with apples that are easily picked from the branches or from the ground. Sounds like a great way to be a farmer.

The problem with apple orchards is not what is seen but what cannot be seen. There are two issues, one controllable with consequences and one can only be managed with difficulty. The former are the wide variety of insect pests that are elusive, difficult to detect, and can destroy apples from the inside-out so that great looking apples are in fact infested and little more than waste. Farmers must understand the pests in their orchards, understand pest biology, and determine what pesticides to apply and when to deal with specific pests. Apple orchards are among the most intensely agrochemical-treated crops with, on average, more than 30 pesticide applications per year.

The other problem with apple orchards is that they are outside. Farmers cannot control the weather patterns the trees experience though they can mitigate extreme temperature variations with fans and burners. Tough winters and cold, wet springs where warm weather can show up, go away for a while and then reappear wreaks havoc with orchards and result in a significant percentage of crop losses. This weather behavior impacts northern apple orchards as well as orange orchards in northern Florida. Mitigation strategies are costly and not amenable to the many smaller orchards.

Another aspect to the farming of fruit is that it seems that every so often the general public discovers that the age of many fruits and vegetables in their grocery store can be as long as 14 months and that the nutritional and anti-oxidant values are minimal.[a] Much of the fruits and vegetables we buy are stored in controlled environments for up to 12 months or more (how else do you get apples in August?). Apples in the store have an average age of 12–14 months; lettuce is stored for up to a month or more; banana for 14 days; tomatoes for up to 6 weeks; potatoes for 9 months; and carrots for up to 9 months. These controlled environments are cold storage and have controlled atmospheres that slow the aging process. As different regions of the world scale their apple production and logistic services, not only will US producers face rising competition but demand for fresh apples during those times of the year when fresh domestic apples are not available could lead to apples from the southern hemisphere replacing aged domestic apples in stores.

The production of food and protein, from farm to table, is on the leading edge of automation because many of the functions needed to run an autonomous farm are in place. Farm operations are becoming more automated with machinery that run on autopilot and drones that spread fertilizer and can monitor the health of crops. Milking operations can now be automated and the raising of livestock, heretofore a very manual process, can be fully automated even with current technology. The raising of livestock is the last area for the application of basic technologies and even in this area, there exists a patented livestock facility that shows, at least conceptually, how livestock can be raised with no human intervention.[b] We show that most steps in the global food supply in developed countries can be automated to mostly Level 4, including livestock production, and that the time to automation for emerging markets should be much faster than it took developed countries.

---

[a] The science of cold apple storage," Autumn Giles, ModernFarmer.com, 5 August 2013 (http://modernfarmer.com/2013/08/the-science-of-cold-apple-storage/).
[b] Automated animal house," U.S. Patent 6,810,832, 18 September, 2002 (http://patft.uspto.gov/netacgi/nph-Parser?Sect1=PTO2&Sect2=HITOFF&p=1&u=%2Fnetahtml%2FPTO%2Fsearch-bool.html&r=34&f=G&l=50&co1=AND&d=PTXT&s1=kairos&OS=kairos&RS=kairos).

2. Traditional Farming

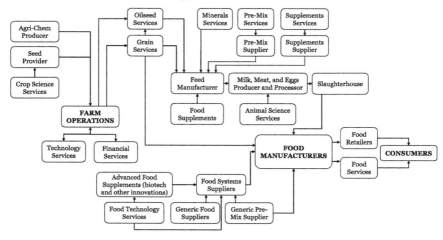

Figure 6.1:　The food supply chains.

There are three main actors in the agriculture supply chain: Farmers, their customers, and their value creation partners (Figure 6.1). The latter assist the Farmer with pre-planting activities such as what crops to plant, how much, machine procurement, financing, pesticides, and logistic services to move these to the farm. The Customer actors are a varied lot of food consumers from distributors to food producers. Most consumers of the actual grains are livestock operations.[c]

The traditional key agricultural functions shown in Figure 6.2 functions are listed below:

1. Crop Management — those agricultural practices used to manage the growth, development, and yield of agricultural crops. The practices used depend on the crops (whether winter or spring crops), the harvested form (e.g., grains, green feed), the planting process, the soil conditions, and weather conditions.

---

[c] "Corn," USDA Economic Research Service, http://www.ers.usda.gov/topics/crops/corn/background.aspx.

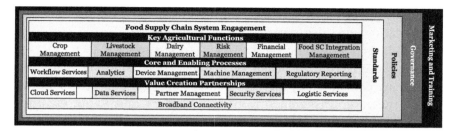

Figure 6.2: Business model for the food supply chain.

2. Livestock Management — those agricultural practices used to manage the growth, development, and yield of livestock (e.g., poultry, cattle, swine).

3. Dairy Management — those agricultural practices used to manage the growth, development, and yield of dairy cows.

4. Risk Management — mostly this is crop and livestock insurance. The enhanced weather forecasting and associated software tools offered have provided farm operations with a heightened sense of awareness of short- and long-duration problems that could occur 10–14 days out.

5. Financial Management — this function is a combination of futures and options markets to hedge agricultural practices as well as financing for machinery, seeds, and other raw materials.

6. Food Supply Chain (SC) Integration Management — the legacy of this function is a highly manual one that involves trucks moving grains, dairy, or livestock from the farm to the grain elevators, dairy processor/distributor, and slaughterhouses.

The Core and Enabling Processes are as follows:

1. Analytics — this is the traditional information captured by the farmer or other data services on the amount of grains planted, livestock size, and dairy production estimates.

2. Machine Management — farms contain a lot of machinery. A farmer can spend a significant amount of time selecting the right machines for a season, get training if necessary, getting

financing, operating and fixing machines. Records on machine operations are also a necessary burden.

3. Regulatory Reporting — the global food supply is so important that the government insists on issuing a vast amount of reports that are consumed by all actors in the supply chain. The raw data for these reports comes from the farmers and value creation partners.

Traditional Value Creation Partnerships are described below:

1. Data Services — traditional key data for a farmer are weather conditions, information on seeds, planting conditions, market pricing of commodities, and so on. The farmer and other actors in the supply chain consume this data at rates ranging from many times per day to once annually.
2. Partner Management — farmers and actors in the supply chain interact. Farmers need to have good relationships with grain merchants/distributors and food manufacturers, and the reverse is also true. These middlemen need to have a trusted source of grains and livestock as well as markets into which they sell their products.
3. Logistic Services — There is a big business in having a truck that can move food supply throughout the supply chain. Many individual farmers have their own trucks to move their output and will provide this service to other farmers. Trucking companies will also move large amounts of output to trains and river barges.

The types of data traditionally important to actors in the food supply chain are shown in Figure 6.3. The functions that are supported by data in the near-term (seconds — 1 month) are generated during the relevant season (daily for dairy operations; weeks to months for the grains or livestock). The farmer has two intense periods of work (planting and harvesting) relative to their other activities and so activities like hedging and crop management can change rapidly. Contract labor used during these intense periods of work help

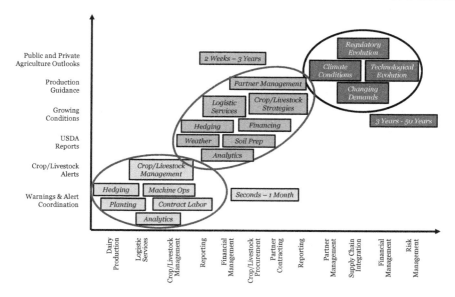

Figure 6.3: Data needed to automate the food supply chain.

with planting though most of the work of contract labor is during harvest season.

On longer timescales, farmers manage risk with weather forecasts and weather-related analytics. For example, in orchards, expectation of cold weather is derived from long-term weather forecasts and analytics based on historical data. This leads to provisioning of heaters and fans to use in those areas of orchards that would be adversely impacted, potential changes to financing (e.g., crop insurance claims with supporting data), and the need for in situ examination of crop damage.

Long-term data that farmers require are more climatic in nature (have we entered a decade of longer cold weather patterns that persist further into the growing season), regulatory (e.g., greater federal government mandates), technological (e.g., GPS), and changing consumer demand (e.g., data on gluten-free evolution in the retail stores).

Livestock management requires continual monitoring of livestock as they grow and it is still a highly manual process relative to crop production. The typical poultry operations involve a long, one-story building that is partially open to the outside to allow venting of enteric and manure emissions so greenhouse gases and other airborne contaminants are not controlled. Dead livestock are disposed of manually and the water supply for the livestock can get contaminated from the air and livestock themselves. Swine and turkeys are raised in similar types of facilities and the process for them is very manual.

The adoption of technology has been minimal for livestock operations relative to crop production. As is described below, more automated solutions do exist but this industry has been highly resistant to change mainly because it is not an area where the producers of the industry are looking for innovation solutions. Everyone is content with status quo in that some growers make money, producers are happy with their margins, and there has been no real change in consumer demand. However, the latter might be seeing changes that are government mandated and would be difficult to manage as it is not just the US government but also foreign governments and NGOs (e.g., the UN).[1,2] Alternatives to livestock products are in the new product development pipeline and include soy-based and seitan-based beef, chicken, and pork. In addition, in vitro beef has been demonstrated and will soon be on the retail market.[d]

3. Autonomous Farming

The future of farming appears to be a service-based model where farmers procure services to create their final product. Autonomous systems have found their way into the farming and downstream systems. It is estimated that the agricultural autonomous system market is expected to grow from $817 million to $16.3 billion by 2020.[e] Typical autonomous systems are driverless farm machinery, milking robots, and drones that operate in the fields and are also capable of

---

[d] "World's first lab-grown burger is eaten in London," http://www.bbc.com/news/science-environment-23576143.

[e] "Robot revolution — Global robot & autonomous system primer," BAML, 16 December 2015.

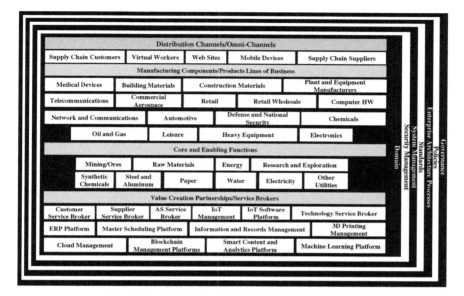

Figure 6.4: New business model for the food supply chains showing those areas that need to be automated.

operating indoors for livestock management work. Overall, the components that need to be in place for a Level 4 farm autonomous operations for crop production (site preparation, planting, mowing, pest management) using drones and driverless machinery are in place (Figure 6.4).

Automation has developed slowly over time as the number of family farms and farmers has decreased, the number of corporate farms has increased, and the productivity of the farms has increased. The use of modern technologies such as computers showed up with Financial Management, Crop Management, and Integration into the larger supply chain. Automation has appeared in specific processes such as Site Preparation, Site Development, and Planting. The infrastructure to support Customer processes (Grain Processors, Merchants, ...) started to accrete automated capabilities in the machinery and computer systems that managed this infrastructure.

Up until around 2000 agriculture was at Level 2. Since then with the rapid technology advancements and GPS most Farmer processes have seen automation development and Crop Management, Analytics, Machine Management, Risk Management, and Financial Management have seen enhanced capabilities based on basic autonomous system techniques.

The new business model has new components to support automated processes:

1. System of Engagement — this must support customers who are autonomous system
2. Blockchain — processes to support a wide variety of blockchain networks that enable M2M transactions.
3. Crowdfunding Services — more and more the ability to support new and innovative ways to raise capital for agricultural purposes. It should enable autonomous system to contribute to this model.

The aforementioned autonomous systems are all composed of sensors collection data (e.g., tractor vision), the rapid collection, processing, and exploitation of data, and autonomous system systems in each component that uses the data to make decisions on timescales ranging from milliseconds to years. The key to fully autonomous farms is integration with its value creation partners and to its customers. The autonomous operations of the value creation partners is similar to those autonomous operations being recognized in manufacturing. Packaging of fertilizer and seed onto driverless trucks and trains is within current technologies and the overall logistic services necessary to get the materials to the right farms at the right times exist today. For customers, a similar autonomous context exists in that these manufacturing environments can be automated with existing technologies or technologies that are soon to be deployed. Basic robotic capabilities are or will be in place to move livestock from truck to freezer. Grains can be moved from the farm to barges on the Mississippi to containers ships in the Gulf of Mexico.

The success to the full automation of the crop production farm is in the integration of those elements of Crop Management,

Financial Management, Device Management, and Machine Management. This integration requires the existence of Workflow Services to tie together all of the areas of the new business model. Right now, this is the purview of human beings and it will be difficult to incorporate their knowledge into an autonomous system that can replicate decision making on crop production. This is where significant value and opportunity lay for innovation and new businesses.

An approach to reaching Level 4 is to break up the autonomous system into three components that are aligned at the data level. AI1 can be focused on domestic and global markets to determine what grains to plant and how much of each. AI2 can be focused on Crop Management and inform AI1 as to the seed types and fertilizers to order. This allows AI1 to negotiate with seed and fertilizers providers on price and delivery. AI2 also informs AI1 on the types of machinery needed and when, based on weather analytics and soil conditions determined by drones that AI2 manages year round. This allows AI1 to negotiate on what equipment is needed and when. AI3 is focused on integration with the rest of the food supply chain. It can begin to determine the best ways to dispose of the crop. This could include storing some on site based on futures pricing and predictions. It could also include negotiating logistic services to move crop to buyers (presumably other AIs) via truck, rail, or truck drones.

4. Autonomous Livestock Production

As aforementioned, an area that has defied significant automation has been in the raising of livestock such as chickens, turkeys, and swine. There does not appear to be much of an incentive for companies to automate livestock production even though there is a value proposition for it. The incentive might not come from the markets but from NGOs and governments given the slow trend that is developing that views livestock production as (1) contributing to climate change and (2) red and processed meat products being viewed as carcinogenic. This trend could very lead to livestock

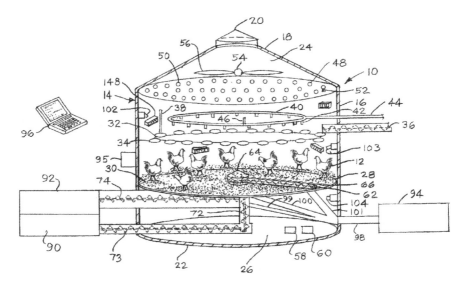

Figure 6.5: A new type of livestock facility to raise any type of livestock.[3]

production being highly regulated and these products becoming more expensive.

Figure 6.5 shows a patented automated livestock facility that demonstrates the efficacy of automating livestock production. The attributes of this facility is that it is a fully automated enclosed growth facility that provides an optimal growing environment while using over 60% less power and emitting 85% less greenhouse gases than existing growth facilities while preventing contamination of water supplies and rivers, has unique ability to function economically year round in any climate or location, and uses common components for growing livestock ranging in size from poultry to cattle thereby allowing a grower options in selecting which type of livestock to grow and when to grow them. Further details and references are in the patent filing.

Private conversations with the patent holder indicates that the design has evolved significantly from this patent filing and is now at a point where designs exist for fully autonomous operation that uses a plethora of sensors that generate data on livestock health, size and weight, air conditions, and manure emissions. The heating and cooling system is used to maintain the optimal temperatures needed throughout the growing process. This system consists of the an HVAC and fan system that works to maintain a uniform air and litter temperature at all times in the house. The outside environment has no impact on the facility. The outside walls are insulated so that interior operations do not interact with the external environment. Therefore, the facility can operate in any climate and geographical location.

The facility has a patented air purifier system to remove air contaminants through a patented self-cleaning ionization system. The system is designed to reduce and/or eliminate air contamination resulting from livestock and requires little or no maintenance because of its patented self-cleaning modules. Field tests have shown that the system purifies the air in adverse conditions from 35% to 55%, lowers operational cost and utility expense by reducing the amount of airflow needed to clean the air, enhances the overall production yield with healthier livestock, and provides cleaner air expulsion into the open community environment.

The manure management process removes manure continually from the bedding material and replaces it with new fresh bedding. This is accomplished using a cleaning arm that picks up the contaminated litter at the front of the arm and moves it to a refurbishment containment facility. At the same time, the cleaning arm deposits clean litter from the back of the arm. The arm moves very slowly to prevent disturbing the poultry. This process also provides a mechanism for the safe removal and processing of dead livestock, which must be isolated from other animal waste. The purifiers and manure management process work together to reduce the greenhouse gas emissions. It is estimated that the facility will reduce greenhouse gas emissions by over 75% and ground water and river water contamination by over 75%.

An LED lighting system provides for the optimal light levels and colors needed throughout the growing process. Research has shown that modification to the light intensity and wavelength during the livestock growth process has a positive impact on production growth. The LED lights can be automatically set to the correct intensity and wavelength over the growth cycle. The LED lights use 90% less energy than the incandescent lights currently used in poultry houses.

There is even an automated capture of livestock that safely moves them into cages for transport to a processor. This provides a higher level of efficiency and safety for the farm worker and livestock, which also allow the house to be emptied and readied for the next livestock more quickly. The transport can take the livestock to an automated slaughterhouse for further processing and packaging. Discussions with the patent holder have demonstrated designs for integrating livestock directly with processes that provide young livestock and the slaughter production facilities thereby making a complete automation possible. What this patent shows is that it is possible to automate the growing of livestock in a similar manner that crop production can be automated.

5. Food Safety and Provenance

Food provenance, in its strictness form, means that a consumer/restaurant knows completely where all the food originated that they are preparing and consuming. At this point, it is not possible for a consumer, whether preparing their own food or eating it in a restaurant, to know where the food comes from geographically, when it was picked, what processing was done to it (e.g., freezing or storing in a rich carbon dioxide container), how it was shipped and what the shipping conditions were, and how long it has been in the store or restaurant before being purchased.

The key component to enable food provenance is the blockchain. It is possible to associate a blockchain with a given individual item so that all transactions that have occurred to that item are logged and persist until the item is consumed.

6. The Autonomous Food Supply Chain and Its Impact

The overview in this chapter demonstrates how the production of food can be largely automated over time and should be one of the first supply chains to be a Level 4 automation where machines controlled by a hierarchy of autonomous systems will do the vast majority of the work and make most of the decisions with minimal input from humans. The key is the proper and robust integration between the agriculture functions at a farm and the external integration of the farm functions with value creation partners such as grain merchants/processors and food manufacturers.

The logistics services are already becoming highly automated.[4] Further evolution of the autonomous truck operations should allow trucks to be loaded at farms by autonomous machinery and loaded/unloaded at grain merchants or slaughterhouses. These processors/distributors can then load the autonomous trucks and the content of the truck can tell the truck where to take it. One can imagine that the truck drones could begin to dominate livestock and frozen meat transport when and if the truck drones become cost competitive to autonomous trucking. The latter will be less expensive to operate before 2020 and therefore there is the expectation that trucking will start to move toward more autonomous operations. The slaughterhouse is becoming more automated and this has resulted in a reduction in the overall workforce that traditionally services this business.

An opportunity for autonomous operations is that the actors in the supply chain can be more proactive in pricing their output for sale. For example, a farmer can position their output on autonomous trucks and while the trucks heads east, look for the best price for the payload and once identified, direct the trucks to that buyer or buyers. This allows the farmer to leverage the markets to hedge their payloads for longer and better knowledge of the market based on bids they have received. Another actor, the meat processor, can advertise beef and the provenance behind it and deliver directly to the consumer via automated trucks and/or small delivery drones. This integration of the food supply chain allows the consumer to ensure they are receiving a product whose provenance is known and receiving it at a time where the food has not been too processed.

The autonomous farm operating at Level 4 appears doable and within 20 years. What are the impacts of a critical mass of autonomous farms? Can these increase food production 70% to feed the

9.6 billion inhabitants of Earth by 2050? Can autonomous farms help in the developing world? Are they immune to man-made security risks and existential risks?

The interaction of AI1s from farms globally has the possibility of rationalizing what is produced, where, and how much. A huge gain in efficiency would be if AI1s coordinated, in some manner, what their production would be while maximizing their profit goal. This is especially true with raising livestock where decisions are sometimes made years earlier. Key areas that autonomous farms could address would be the huge amount of food waste that occurs today, currently estimated to be 30%, as well as better management of existential risks. For example, the climate at each farm world-wide would allow for climate maps to be posted and made available to AI1, AI2, and AI3 for their decision making. If drought conditions were identified in areas of the Midwest based on data provided by each farm, interactions of farms' AI1s could rationalize what is planted when and where. Based on financial goals, AI1s may decide to inform AI2s of incoming droughts and that the AI1s have negotiated who will grow what crops. The AI2 will then take into account the drought when planting and managing crop production.

The possibility exists that a direct line of sight from consumer demand to agricultural output, if it could exist, would drive greater efficiencies into global autonomous farm operations. Restaurants could pay for crops sourced from specific organic farms and pay for that privilege with same day delivery via aerial drone or driverless car. Consumers could buy certain crops from farms, even identifying the plants they want their vegetables from, and have them delivered to them via drone delivery in one day from the farm. The possibility exists for small family farms that typically participate in local farmer's markets to advertise their produce and have them delivered by aerial drone or driverless cars in a larger geographical area. The implication is that food distributors and grocery stores could be marginalized. Just like the milkman of the twentieth century delivered milk every morning, aerial drones or your driverless car could provide the daily or weekly supply of fresh fruits, vegetables, meats, and other foods.

Opportunities abound for new business models in the integration of the food supply chain though the pre-requisites are substantial. While automation of individual farm operations, value-creation partners, and customers is underway, who is incented to integrate them? One example is Cargill who has a presence in most aspects of the food supply chain and can provide provenance to consumers.[5] Cargill's business model is an example of a model that could transform itself into a fully autonomous operation sooner than other types of business models. Cargill is positioned to implement a workflow process governed by AI1, AI2, and AI3 to automate farm operations and integrate that with their downstream activities of grain merchant, food processor, and food packager. For restaurants and consumers, Cargill could use Amazon as the fulfillment service to advertise the food they grow and where, allow customers to buy produce (deliver a dozen catfish from this fish pond), and Amazon will deliver the fish via drone. Customers could even buy futures on the fish in certain ponds that have a large number of likes on Facebook.

This overall architecture would allow AIs representing consumers and businesses to buy and sell foods easily. Consider the use of a Facebook-type capability where sources of food with well-defined data about what is grown there (crops or protein), restaurants with their needs well-defined, and fulfillment services such as Amazon come together. The AIs could negotiate with each other for fulfillment of demand and delivery with reputational data posted there for each side of the transaction to take into consideration. Such a process would need the blockchain and smart contract capabilities to ensure the integrity of the source of food, the identity of the consumer, and fulfillment of the transaction.

It is also clear that there will be a reduced need over time for humans in the food supply chain. Over time, humans would slowly be removed as autonomous system capabilities become more significant. The presence of humans should persist in those integration points in the supply chain. These include ensuring the correct operation of any autonomous system (is the autonomous system truly satisfying its goals or is it losing its way?) and that financial and physical handoffs are occurring.

The automation of the food supply chain carries with it the possibility that the government could exert total governance over it. The government could, if it chose, take over defining the goals and outcomes for the AIs. Many countries in the past have tried central planning with mixed results. The automation of a food supply chain provides countries and NGOs with the ability to take control of food and livestock production and ensure that their goals are met instead of general market forces. A government or NGO could define the data and metadata that govern decisions of what is grown, when, and where. They could control or at least have access to the Workflow Services to ensure that their mandates are met. In effect the global food supply is turned into a regulated utility.

Another challenge of the new food supply chain business model is Security Services. How can security be implemented at the level of Workflow Services? The use of the blockchain and smart contracts is mandatory. However, given past experiences, it will take years for the impact of hackers that work to disrupt the autonomous operations to be minimized. The clear targets for hackers will be the driverless farm machinery and those used in Logistic Services. Their targets are driverless cars today so there is every reason to believe they will see their counterparts in the food supply chain attacked with equal vigor. The one difference here is that the logistic services involve non-human cargoes so hackers will have no problem crashing a truck into a river or a truck drone into a lake where no human injuries occur.

The challenge for automation of the global food supply chain is not so much in the automation of an individual farm, regardless if that farm produces grains, milk, vegetables, or livestock. The world is clearly moving in that direction and it is safe to assume that farms will be largely hands-off within 10 years. The challenge is the integration of elements of the supply chain where metadata, data including financial data, and data describing the condition of the product are exchanged (either freely or paid) and used to manage other parts of the supply chain. Who is incented to make this happen? Companies like Cargill? In the absence of such stakeholders, governments and NGOs could easily step in and assume control.

References

1. Bouvard, V *et al.* (2015). Carcinogenicity of consumption of red and processed meat. *Lancet Oncol*, 16(16), 1599–1600.
2. Goodland, R and J Anhang (November/December 2009). Livestock and climate change. *World Watch Magazine*, Volume 22, No. 6.
3. Kairos, L.L.C., "Automated animal house", U.S. Patent 6,810,832, issued November 2, 2004, used by permission.
4. Davies, A (5 May 2015). The world's first self-driving semi-truck hits the road. Wired. http://www.wired.com/2015/05/worlds-first-self-driving-semi-truck-hits-road/.
5. Bunge, J (7 April 2016). Cargill's new place in the food chain. *The Wall Street Journal*.

CHAPTER 7

Logistics

1. Introduction

Ever wonder why things are a certain size? Why is a solid rocket booster like the ones that powered the Space Shuttle and are part of the Space Launch System 12 feet wide and not 14 feet or 20 feet? Wide is better to store more propellant and increase thrust. Why are tractor trailers less than 14 feet in height? If they were higher they could carry more and be more profitable? Why does Caterpillar ship its large bulldozers in pieces and assemble them on-site and not at the factory? Things are a certain size and no more due to restrictions on the logistics of moving materiel. Tractor trailers are restricted in height by the vertical clearance of overpasses on interstates and other highway systems. They have to be less than 14 feet if they expect to travel under all of the overpasses present on the interstate highway system. Materiel moved by rail are restricted in dimensionality by the size of the train gauge used throughout the United States, which is 4 feet 8 inches, and whose origin dates to the earliest English railroads.[a] This restricts the effective width of rail payloads to less than

---

[a] Baxter B (1966). *Stone Blocks and Iron Rails (Tramroads). Industrial Archaeology of the British Isles.* Newton Abbot: David & Charles. It is possible to create a line of sight from this track gauge to the width of two horses that powered a Roman chariot as these chariots created ruts about 5 ft wide. It appears this gauge size has

12 feet and the solid rocket boosters, which are transported by rail, are about as wide a payload that can be accommodated by rail transport. Therefore, choices made for good reasons impose restrictions on the physical dimensions and weights of what the world manufactures and moves.[b]

Is it possible to relieve these constraints? Yes it is but it must also be emphasized the above constraints are not going away. Logistical services are undergoing change because the thing they support, namely the supply chains across many industries, are undergoing change.[c] A new transport mode will make an impact but the traditional transport modes will also change in ways to transform logistics.[1]

Logistic services companies should be the first to being operating pilotless aircraft and ground vehicles for a simple reason. To put it bluntly, if a FedEx 767 pilotless aircraft crashes on a Mississippi farm after takeoff from Memphis, how big a deal is that? No humans were harmed, the airplane is insured, and FedEx will probably pay to restore the farm. The cargo is lost but large parts of the cargo can be reproduced and new copies sent. The same holds for trones and potential new modes of transportation like the Hyperloop (discussed below). In short, logistic services that transport cargo offers to be the guinea pig, the first adopter of autonomous system that can be used to make autonomous system commercial operations much more safe and easier so that when a certain safety level is reached, humans can be assured that the autonomous system will have millions of hours of testing completed. The autonomous system logistic operations will have sampled the many bad and ugly operational situations, figured out how to deal with these, and bring a level of safety to routine operations near aircraft safety today.

---

more to do with the preferences of George Stephenson, the English civil engineer who built the first public intercity railway line in the world to use steam locomotives, than anything else.

[b] It is possible to move objects that cannot be moved via road or rail via aircraft such as a 747. Such modals are rare relative to materiel moved by trucks and rail and therefore not relevant to this discussion.

[c] 2016 commercial transportation trends, strategy&, PWC.com, http://www.strategyand.pwc.com/perspectives/2016-commercial-transportation-trends

There seems to be this belief that people will not fly in planes with no pilots. What if the airline offered a $99 round trip business class fare between New York and Beijing? The three largest categories of cost for an airline are aircraft, fuel, and labor. Fuel and labor are over 50%. Creative financing helps with acquiring aircraft. Fuel can be hedged, or in the case of Delta, an airline can buy their own refinery to ensure a consistent and manageable supply of fuel. The one area that has been challenging for airlines are labor costs which are about 25%.[d] What happens to an airline if it can reduce its labor costs by 90%? This is a huge value proposition for the airlines and may be significant enough that airlines would form a joint venture to purchase a logistics company and move to start flying pilotless aircraft at the earliest opportunity. Profit margins certainly increase but the airlines have greater pricing flexibility.

There is a growing consensus that driverless trucks are inevitable. Truck transport is a commodity business with 25 million trucks operating in the United States, over 5 million truck drivers, and about 1.2 million trucking companies.[2] 90% of these companies operate six or fewer trucks. And the reason is simple: there is money in operating a fleet of driverless trucks and removing the human driver. Operating costs are one aspect but safety is another. The US government estimates the costs of truck collisions at $87 billion a year, with 116,000 people either killed or injured. The expectation is that driverless trucks will significantly reduce these numbers.

Driverless trucks can be tested and matured just as cargo companies can test pilotless aircraft (see below). One example is the surface mines of Rio Tinto in Australia. Rio Tinto has deployed driver trucks at its mines that have currently covered almost 5 million km moving mined materials from the mine egress to the transportation hubs. The knowledge captured by Rio Tinto and Caterpillar is of great value because that information and remote operations competencies developed over these 5 million km can be monetized to other driverless truck operators.

---

[d] This number comes from analysis of SEC filings from the top ten publically traded airlines.

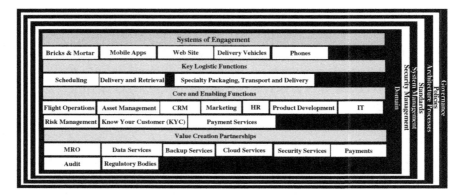

Figure 7.1: The current business model for a logistics company.

Figure 7.1 shows the current business model (generic) for a logistics company to support its inter-modal delivery capabilities:

1. Systems of Engagement — this layer manages the interactions with the customers, whether commercial or retail. These interactions can take place in a traditional storefront location or with newer technologies.

The Key Logistic Functions are as follows:

1. Scheduling — process to allocate resources over multiple time frames to accomplish specific tasks.
2. Delivery and Retrieval — process to allocate resources to move services or products. This includes availability, convenience, courtesy, safety, accuracy, reliability, speed, and dependability.
3. Specialty Product Transport and Packaging — Logistics companies deliver more than packages. Sometimes those packages are animals or large convention displays. These require special packaging, pricing, and quality control.

The Core and Enabling Processes are listed below:

1. Flight Operations — the unique aspect of flying cargo planes is subject to FAA regulations. Therefore, logistics companies tend to have a separate business unit whose sole function is to provide flight services to the rest of the company.

2. Asset Management — processes to support the lifecycle of tangible and intangible assets.
3. CRM — processes to support customer relationship management including problem resolution, new customer acquisition, and customer retention.
4. Marketing — processes to support the communication between the logistics company and its retail and commercial customers.
5. HR — processes to support the management of people in the logistics company especially around policies and procedures.
6. Product Development — processes to support the development of innovation, new product development, and transition of products to an operational mode.
7. IT — processes to support the technology strategies, design, build, test, and run at all levels.
8. Risk Management — the implicit and explicit risks that are finite or persistent.
9. Know Your Customer (KYC) — processes to verify the identity of a customer especially with regards to recent and very prescriptive regulations.
10. Payment Services — processes to support the myriad of ways banks can receive and send payments (e.g., credit cards, debit cards, PayPal).

Traditional Value Creation Partnerships are described below:

1. MRO — Companies that provide maintenance, repair, and overhaul services for the various fleets a logistics company uses.
2. Data Services — companies that provide data feeds (e.g., market data) and document retention services.
3. Backup Services — companies that enable frequent and deep backups and business continuity services.
4. Cloud Services — companies that provide public and hybrid cloud services.
5. Security Services — companies that provide physical security, network security monitoring, and penetration analysis.
6. Payments — credit card companies, PayPal, SWIFT, and other payment channels.

7. Audit — external auditors, forensic auditors, and other companies' deep-dive services into operations.
8. Regulatory Bodies — these are the various local, state, and federal regulatory agencies a bank deals with on a regular basis.
   More and more this might include supranational agencies.

2. It Is All About the Trone (and the Hyperloop?)

When people think of drones they think of the small quadcopters or
the large drones seen on TV used to patrol borders and in theaters
of war. There are a myriad of shapes and sizes but none as large and
functional as manned aircraft and heavy lift helicopters. Some of the
smallest drones known are generically called wallet drones and can
fit inside a pocket and be charged there.[e] The military is working on
aerial drones that are similar in size to very small insects. There are
underwater drones that are being built to swim like a fish and to
hibernate on the seabed near strategically important sites in the event
they are needed. Aerial, ground-based, and submersible drones have
been and will continue to take the place of manned aircraft, vehicles,
and submarines.[3] We also know that driverless cars and driverless
trucks are in the works.[f]

As of 2016, small quadcopter drones can handle payloads up to
100 pounds. Eventually, drones that can take the place of a truck or
railroad car and fly that payload to whatever destination is required
will become available if current trends continue in size and capabilities. An outcome of these trends within 15 years are quadcopters
that can carry payloads similar to those carried by tractor trailers
and possibly even railroad cars. Trucks can carry up to 50,000 of
payload and a boxcar can carry over 200,000 pounds. These truck
drones, or trones for short, will be able to replace trucks on the road
and railroad cars as long as they are cost competitive and offer value-
added services.

---

[e] AERIX DRONES, Aerix Wallet Drone — World's smallest quadcopter, http://
aerixdrones.com/products/axis-wallet-drone?variant=1299813288
[f] Autonomous car, https://en.wikipedia.org/wiki/Autonomous_car

A key advantage is that materiel being moved by trones is not restricted as the materiel that is moved by truck or rail. Engineering designs of almost every product produced are restricted by the height of an overpass or the train gauge. If those logistic constraints were removed, then companies would be free to create unrestricted product designs and begin incorporating these design changes into their products. An argument against the use of trones is that the installed based on manufacturers will preclude a move to unrestricted sizes; factories do not have the machinery to build unrestricted products, so therefore none will. This objection becomes less relevant when 3D printers are used in greater numbers.

Another benefit of a trone is that unlike a tractor-trailer or a rail car, a trone does not have to use existing infrastructure to operate. A tractor-trailer needs roads and a rail car needs tracks and a train engine. There are still areas of the United States whose roads cannot accommodate trucks and the minimally required infrastructures certainly do not exist in developing countries. Infrastructure also does not exist when a catastrophe has occurred and roads are impassable and bridges down.

The fact that Trones and drones like the ones that Amazon will use for delivery will fly over much of the United States, they can perform value-added surveillance using video, broadband images, and hyperspectral imaging. The data they obtain will be of value to insurance companies, the government, construction firms, retailers, and many other industries. The trone can actually decide to sell the data on its own to humans and to other autonomous system.

We discuss the use of autonomous systems in Section 8.6 for the insurance industry and how autonomous drones can assist with property risk management and catastrophic events. We discuss here the use of trones for similar catastrophes. Logistic services to assist in a catastrophic event like a hurricane, earthquake, tornado, or major storms can be problematic. It can take days to move the necessary supplies into an impacted region and remove debris in all its forms from the impacted region. The days and weeks after a catastrophic event is dangerous to first responders as they seek survivors and attempt to clear and repair infrastructure so that supplies can be brought in to execute further repairs. Recent events have provided the rationale for designing and testing autonomous systems to be used as first responders.[g] The Defense Advanced Research Projects Agency (DARPA) created the Robotics Challenge to *"accelerate progress in robotics and hasten the day when robots have sufficient dexterity and robustness to enter areas too dangerous for humans and mitigate the impacts of natural or man-made disasters."* The impetus came from lessons learned after the nuclear disaster at Fukushima, Japan, in 2011. The need for autonomous systems to deliver robots into the impacted areas so that the robots could enter the nuclear plant and effect repairs was clearly demonstrated.

On August 13, 2013, Elon Musk announced the Hyperloop. This idea has a long and well-developed history.[h] This current effort benefited from a group of engineers focused on nothing else but this idea to provide an initial concept with enough details to pass an initial sanity check.[4] To their credit, SpaceX put all of the Hyperloop designs into open source and this has resulted in a number of new companies starting up to explore development of the key technologies. The Hyperloop is a tube in which the pressure is reduced relative to the outside atmosphere so that inside the tube there is a partial vacuum. A pod carrying cargo and/or people moves through the tube on a cushion of air at speeds approaching a commercial airliner. The initial estimates are that a pod traveling from Los Angeles to San Francisco should take about 35 min.

The Hyperloop is an autonomous system and conceptually is capable of carrying substantial amounts of cargo and humans. It could move cargo from ports to major transportation hubs to be put on planes, long-haul trucks, or trains. Since the announcement, a number of companies have started to prove out the idea including building small lengths of tubes to test the technologies and integrated systems.[5] The work is progressing from the bottom up with key components being tested first, with the first integrated system

---

[g] DARPA Robotics Challenge (DRC), US Defense Advanced Research Projects Agency, 2015, http://www.theroboticschallenge.org/
[h] HyperLoop, https://en.wikipedia.org/wiki/Hyperloop

test scheduled to be done sometime in the next 2 years. Planning work is being done for a route between Stockholm and Helsinki and with Slovakia.

The Hyperloop is a potential autonomous system that would move the logistics services to a higher level of complete autonomy faster than without it. It is clear that driverless cars, driverless trucks, and trones will move Logistics to greater autonomy. Planes, trains, and trucks can move cargo from ports to large transportation hubs to small transportation hubs. Trucks and trones can move cargo from point to point, initially small distances and at some point the trone can be used for long-haul transport. Therefore, there is line of sight to Level 3 autonomy quickly and then to Level 4 before other industries.

An unintended side effect of the Hyperloop effort is that it gathers data on how the government and NGOs will respond to change. The trone, pilotless aircraft, driverless cars and trucks have their impact which is described herein. The Hyperloop is different in that its impact is more about infrastructure impact than just replacing humans. Impacting infrastructure means impacting political interests, NGO interests, and a myriad of other interests who tend to use the political processes to their advantage. This is not a pejorative statement, just a statement of fact. Regardless of how perceived as good, bad, or ugly, the current environment has produced a superior transportation system relative to the rest of the world. But is it an environment conducive to change? That depends where one is. The State of California is building a conventional rail system called the California High Speed Rail that is an infrastructure project that is not just a construction challenge but has many stakeholders who are sensitive to changes or competition. Already there have been statements that the Hyperloop will never work or cost 10–100 times its estimate. Basically, the claim is that the high-speed rail envisioned for California is a better alternative. This has not stopped work from progressing in the state to developing the Hyperloop though it is clear the regulatory hurdles to building an operational version of it will be considerable. The State of Texas which does not have a similar high-speed rail system in the works has welcomed Hyperloop prototypes. Several companies have been established to pursue taking the next steps in proving out the technologies.

The final thing to watch for something like the Hyperloop autonomous system is this: will it be the first large-scale infrastructure project that does not require public funding and is built 90% with private funding? No other project such as an interstate highway or other public transportation systems has been financed using private investment funds. The Hyperloop does offer that possibility. Can it happen? Of course, given the concentrated wealth in the United States and the ability to raise funds online. Will it happen? Again, this will be an unintended consequence of the Hyperloop in that its very existence will provide data on how the local, state, and federal governments will respond to change. There are many reasons why governments want to control the funding of an infrastructure project so even though a Hyperloop might be expensive, government may still insist on funding it or large parts of it so it can be regulated and satisfy their needs for tax revenues and respect for the political process.

Figure 7.2 shows a new automated logistics business model. The key is that logistics integrates the supply chains for a variety of

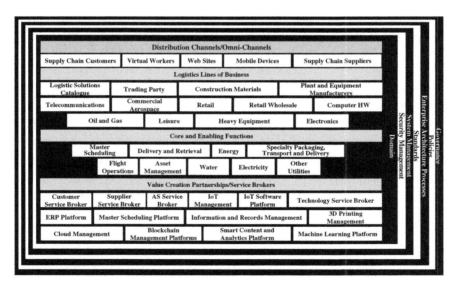

Figure 7.2: New business model for the logistics business showing those areas that need to be automated.

industries using common elements and services. Logistics companies are also the best entity to maintain the blockchain for supply chain partners. It can be the only AS that has complete visibility across all elements and geographies. The nature of the Flight Operations changes significantly due to the inclusion of drones and trones. It is unclear if an organization that manages normal human-based flights can also manage unmanned flight operations. The military has separated manned and unmanned flight operations for good reasons. MRO will be different as well as there need to be competencies in small, medium, large, and 747-sized unmanned aerial vehicles.

The data (Fig. 7.3) show that the AS for logistics will need to determine how to fuse data from multiple timescales to create effective AS. Logistics depends heavily on infrastructure data on how to plan and scheduled transports. More and more weather and climate data impacts the requirements of the supply chain partners and shipping. The master schedule governing a supply chain that supports a variety of AS will need data from all timescales.

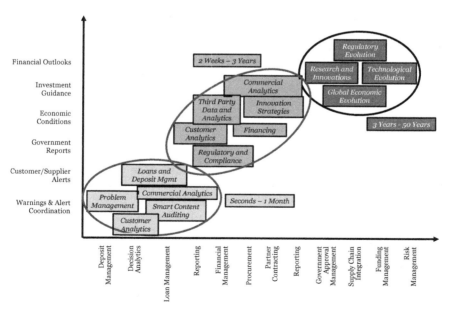

Figure 7.3: Data needed to automate the new logistics business.

Table 7.1: Opportunities for big data in logistic services.

	New Capabilities	As Is Analysis	Management Horizon	Strategic Horizon
Logistics	System of Engagement	• Pilot Robo-Advisors	• Pilot M2M transactions with Robo-Advisors	• Enable autonomous system to perform a majority of Key Logistic Functions
	Robo-Advisors	• Leverage existing providers • Integration into mobile devices	• Customer personalization • Breadth and Depth Enhancement • Richer customer interactions	• Product Research • On-demand presence • Rich interactions with other autonomous system
	Blockchain Services	• Familiarization	• Pilot projects for use in basic processes and automation of internal manual processes	• Long-term monitoring by autonomous system of properties and humans • Transaction management

3. Impact of Autonomous Logistic Services

Many of the business models discussed in this book rely on a logistic service to provide delivery of goods and possibly supply chain management solutions. If that service becomes Level 3 or Level 4, it would enable a transformation of how supply chains work and induce changes to the business models of the myriad of companies in many industrial sectors. The bottom-line is that autonomous systems in logistic services will enable on-demand movement of materiel between any two points without regard to natural and man-made restrictions. Logistic services that support the food supply chain, manufacturing, and retail should reach Levels 3 and 4 on a timescale faster than most of parts of these respective supply chains. Table 7.1 illustrates the opportunities of analytics in the logistical services.

There is one last, admittedly a little out there, comment to make about autonomous logistic services. There is a lot of discussion about manned cars and trucks being replaced with driverless versions. We have also discussed the evolution of a heavy lift drone called a trone that can replace a truck and railroad car and not only provide more efficient logistical services but also help remove constraints on engineering designs imposed by the limitations of the railroad and superhighways. This begs the question: Will humans find car aerial drones that leverage miniaturized versions of the trone technology as acceptable solutions? There has always been a desire for personal flying and submersible cars since Little Nellie appeared in the James Bond film "You Only Live Twice."

References

1. Morris, B (14 April 2016). E-Commerce boom roils trucking industry. *The Wall Street Journal.* http://www.wsj.com/articles/e-commerce-boom-roils-trucking-industry-1459442027
2. Berman, DK (23 July 2013). Daddy, what was a truck driver?. *The Wall Street Journal.* http://www.wsj.com/articles/SB100014241278873 24144304578624221804774116
3. Rutkin, A (8 May 2015). Autonomous truck cleared to drive on US roads for the first time. *New Scientist.* https://www.newscientist.com/article/dn27485-autonomous-truck-cleared-to-drive-on-us-roads-for-the-first-time/
4. Musk, E (12 August 2013). Hyperloop alpha. *SpaceX.* http://www.spacex.com/sites/spacex/files/hyperloop_alpha-20130812.pdf
5. Wells, G (11 May 2016). Hyperloop One accelerates toward future with high-speed test. *The Wall Street Journal.* http://www.wsj.com/articles/hyperloop-one-accelerates-towards-future-with-high-speed-test-1462960803

CHAPTER 8

Financial Services

1. Introduction

The traditional banking business model where banks depend on deposits and loans for their income is becoming less relevant. Banks that depend on this traditional model will need to change or develop and exit strategy. The death of the bank bricks and mortar has been predicted for many years and may still happen. However, whether or not banks have a physical presence as significant as they have now is less important to their survival than the business model their online presence and bricks and mortar capabilities support. The idea of digitization of financial services means that most banking and insurance processes are automated. As each process is digitized it can become its own AS. Banks will need to provide new and alternative services for their retail and commercial customers. Insurance companies will need to develop products that insure automated processes which means that commercial customers become more important. This impacts companies whose dominant customer is the retail customer but due to automation, consumers will have less of a need of insurance.

We began this book with a description of a highly evolved autonomous system, namely a high-frequency trading system or HFT. Every day, over $5 trillion is traded in the currency markets. This dwarfs the stock exchanges by at least an order of magnitude.

Taken all together globally, around $6 trillion is traded daily with the vast majority done by computers. Financial services is far more automated than most other industries but that automation is not evident to the general public. The general public sees a mortgage process that is the same as it was 30 years ago; only now, there are more documents to sign and stronger underwriting requirements including the source of the money being used for the down payment. On the other hand, they are using electronic payments in greater numbers with online applications, allowing them to automate their bill payment services. The past 10 years has seen the number or checks written decline by half and those remaining are cleared autonomously.[a] Cash is still king and there are indications that even its use could be on the wane. The general public sees a government system that has increased the use of regulation to ensure that the problems in the last recession are not repeated. The jury will still be out for years as to whether this sort of intervention will be automated or force more and more manual processes to be executed.

A key process that a financial system supports and facilitates is payments. Banks and other financial institutions act as trusted third parties in financial transactions and provide the trust layer so that both sides of a transaction are confident that the transaction will occur as intended. This trusted third party role has always been the one aspect of a bank that sets it apart from any other entity in the world, including to a certain extent, governments. If this trusted third party role of a bank should disappear, then the value of banks to the rest of society would be diminished and banks would be marginalized, especially those with significant bricks and mortars investments and investments in human capital to execute bank processes.

The blockchain is the one technology that could be that technology that removes the need for a bank as a trusted third party especially among autonomous systems. Banks are incented to maximize the cost of a transaction and keep funds on their books as long as

[a] The 2013 Federal Reserve Payments Study, https://www.frbservices.org/files/communications/pdf/research/2013_payments_study_summary.pdf.

possible, even if it is only overnight. The more steps in a transaction, the more that can be charged and the funds repurposed. The impact of the blockchain to banks is manifold. The first and most obvious is that the need for trusted third parties is removed. The blockchain is the trust machine for present and past transactions. It allows for two parties, unknown to one another, to enter into a transaction where each knows the transaction will occur. The second is financial risk management. The use of the blockchain removes much of the inherent risks in the financial system due to the presence of humans. Risks like counterparty defaults, settlement risk (a well-honed skill in trading pits), and overall systematic risk where a trusted third party defaults can be removed with the proper implementation of a blockchain. The latter is not a foregone conclusion. Many of the start-ups in the blockchain FinTech field are financed by traditional financial institutions. The blockchain will be implemented so as to maintain their leadership and profits which is how previous technologies were implemented. The latter could have automated the financial processes far more than they are today but the implementers chose not to do so. Expect the same dynamic to occur with the blockchain.

2. The End of Human-to-Human Interactions

There is a line of sight to the end of the brick and mortar bank location and the problem is that (1) it shows up in many different ways and (2) society as a whole is getting more comfortable with electronic banking.

How do you know that when you are talking on the phone with someone or chatting with a customer service representative on the phone that you are interacting with a human? Jill Watson was the name of a graduate assistant for an online course at Georgia Tech. None of the students met her but they interacted with her and had a positive experience. Turns out Jill Watson was a new use of the IBM Watson technology applied to the educational setting.[1] This simple example is the start of how autonomous systems will ingratiate themselves into our lives.

1. Systems of Engagement — this layer manages the interactions with the customers, whether commercial or retail. These interactions can take place in a traditional banking location or with newer technologies.

The Key Banking Functions are as follows:

1. Retail Banking — processes to support tellers, cash management, 401 Ks, IRAs, safe deposit boxes, and other services traditionally used by humans whose net worth does not exceed a certain threshold.
2. Commercial Banking — processes to support businesses and non-profits. This includes lines of credit, money at call, credit card processing, overdraft management, bill discounting, and demand and term loans.
3. Private Banking and Wealth Management — processes to support banking, investment, and other financial services provided by banks to individuals with net worth in excess of $1 million.
4. Loans — processes to support car loans, mortgages, and various commercial loans.
5. Treasury Services — processes to support accounts payable, accounts receivable, liquidity management, reporting, and trade finance.

The Core and Enabling Processes are listed below:

1. Enterprise Risk — the framework under which a financial institution manages various areas of risk. This also defines a risk-based approach to managing the enterprise.[2]
2. Asset Management — processes to support the life cycle of tangible and intangible assets.
3. CRM — processes to support customer relationship management including problem resolution, new customer acquisition, and customer retention.
4. Marketing — processes to support the communication between the financial institution and its retail and commercial customers.

5. HR — processes to support the management of people in the financial institution, especially around policies and procedures.
6. Product Development — processes to support the development of innovation, new product development, and transition of products to an operational mode.
7. IT — processes to support the technology strategies, design, build, test, and run at all levels.
8. Risk Management — the implicit and explicit risks that are finite or persistent.
9. Know Your Customer (KYC) — processes to verify the identity of a customer, especially with regards to recent and very pre-scriptive banking regulations.
10. Payment Services — processes to support the myriad of ways banks can receive and send payments (e.g., credit cards, debit cards, PayPal).
11. Deposit and Loan Management — processes to support the deposits made to the bank from various payment services and to support various loan products.

Traditional Value Creation Partnerships are described below:

1. Loan Processors — companies that provide loan collection and processing services.
2. Data Services — companies that provide data feeds (e.g., market data) and document retention services.
3. Backup Services — companies that enable frequent and deep backups and business continuity services.
4. Cloud Services — companies that provide public and hybrid cloud services.
5. Security Services — companies that provide physical security, network security monitoring, and penetration analysis.
6. Payments — credit card companies, PayPal, SWIFT, and other payment channels.
7. Audit — external auditors, forensic auditors, and other companies deep-dive services into operations.

8. Regulatory Bodies — these are the various local, state, and federal regulatory agencies a bank deals with on a regular basis. More and more of this might include supranational agencies.
9. Investment Management — companies that provide investment services (e.g., managing pensions for commercial customers).

If the various functions are broken down to more granular levels, it is clear that more and more of these granular functions are manual in nature. Multiple assessments of banking processes shows not just manual processes are prevalent, but that these processes could be automated but are not. There are several reasons for this. First and foremost are the regulators who can be ad hoc and irregular in their audits and assessments of banking operations. A bank can automate most of its loan processing but regulators typically find issues with loan processing and it is difficult to hide behind an autonomous system. Banks find it easier to have humans manage processes that tend to attract the attention of regulators to ensure problems are addressed or can be explained away. An autonomous system cannot convince a regulator that a perceived problem is not a problem.

A second reason for manual processes is that over the past decades, banks have implemented new systems whose original intent was to provide a complete computer solution to a business process. Typically, this is undertaken at the behest of a vendor selling their shiny bright object to banks. The banks want to relieve their continuing processing pain and problems and view these shiny new objects as a complete solution. The issue is that these solutions are rarely complete. The dynamics of large IT projects is that for a complete solution to be implemented, all phases of the implementation must be completed. This almost never happens. For example, suppose there are three phases to the implementation of a new solution. There are seven success criteria to any implementation: (1) leadership support and the maintenance of that support; (2) phased implementations; (3) strong scope management; (4) effective project management; (5) implementing the solution on a mature enterprise architecture; (6) effective change management; and (7) issues management where issues are actually dealt with the first time and never reappear. A project will start off with great fanfare and kickoff meetings between the project team, leadership, and external vendors(s). Projects can implement functionality to replace the low hanging fruit. Typically, the first few releases do show success and drive the desire for greater and greater functionality. The final deliveries for Phase 1 can have more to them than originally envisioned and this makes stakeholders happy but not the financial groups as more functionality means higher costs from vendors and staff who labored to get the Phase 1 solution implemented and operational. Inevitably, Phase 2 gets de-scoped to keep the project on budget. Over time the project becomes just another project and not the shiny new bight object because something else has replaced it in that category. Leadership support begins to wane and people want to move onto other more interesting projects. Phase 2 can use up most of the remaining budget to implement a fraction of what was originally intended. Phase 3 never gets done.

The impact of this failure is that those processes that were supposed to be implemented, such as exception reporting, continue to be manual and in fact increases in workload because this old shiny new object generates exception reporting whose resolution was intended to be automatic but is now just given to this outsourced organization to deal with so the project leaders can declare victory and move on. Because this dynamic of incomplete implementations occurs multiple times over several decades and corporate memory is short, banks find it difficult to remove this accreted mess and in order to maintain it all end up implementing integration services to ensure all the legacy systems function and provide continued value to what banking function they support.

The availability of robo-advisors is a next step toward the automation of financial services.[3] Robo-advisors use websites with embedded AI software to put investors into asset allocation plans that meet their various financial goals with a minimal amount of information from the human. They can be considered autonomous systems. Their information comes from website interactions with the humans, capture of market and news information, and it makes decisions and acts on its own to manage portfolios. The use of robo-advisors has grown from $10 million of assets under management to close to $10 billion. Several start-ups in this area claim they are growing their assets 400% per year as more and more people move new money and existing 401 Ks and IRAs into accounts managed by robo-advisors. A key value proposition that robo-advisors offer is that minimum account size can be a few thousand dollars and not the $1 million minimum some wealth advisors require. In addition, like many other financial services firms, these robo-advisors are offering to aggregate a client's many credit cards, mortgages, loans, and other assets into a dashboard for them to manage.

The success of robo-advisors to date cannot be lost on financial services firms but yet it appears the industry view is that these robo-advisors are a flash in the pan type of technology. In their view, they believe people will tire of the lack of human interactions and return to the fold. A conversation with several wealth management firms indicates they do not see a risk to robo-advisors but as just another attempt to capture people's assets and then eventually there will be humans who will get involved. They point to what Charles Schwab was initially and what it is now as well as the Internet pure plays such as Discover brokerage Direct that were absorbed into Morgan Stanley Dean Winter and used for their retail customers. Now these Internet pure plays are just part of what financial advisors offer their $1 million+ customers.

The difference with robo-advisors is that even if they are absorbed into a wealth management firm, they are the first autonomous system in this field that can legitimately replace a financial advisor. The Internet pure plays did not have this ability nor did the early Charles Schwab. These robo-advisors are accreting greater and greater functionality so they can perform faster and better for the client than any traditional financial advisor. One of the reasons for this is that a robo-advisor can by-pass the legacy systems that have built up over time at wealth management firms. A generic picture of the wealth management business model with the following changes as compared to banking business model:

1. Sales — wealth management firms are proactive in pursuing high net worth individuals first and foremost. These are a customer

segment that requires human relationships. The retail segment is pursued via marketing using online, social media, and TV.

2. Trading Platform — typically a sophisticated application that allows a customer to manage their portfolio.
3. Clearing and Settlement — these processes support activities from the time a commitment is made for a transaction until the transaction assets (e.g., securities) are delivered.

The thing to recognize here is that this architecture is a mass of accretion built up over time with components that can date back to the mid-1980s. One wealth management firm in particular still has to run some mainframe COBOL programs to service some customers because there is no business case to replace it with the new technologies present in modern CRM and ERP systems.

Over the years, Wealth Management firms spend substantial amounts of money to redo the "broker workstation." The past 40 years have seen new broker workstations created using the latest architectures available (X-Windows on Unix, client/server, Internet, distributed Internet, thick clients, thin clients, mobile, ...). The broker workstations were built to allow brokers and financial advisors to have access to customer accounts and the markets. The problem with these architectures is that typically the old architecture was never removed. The new architecture was built on top of the old one so eventually a Wealth Management company ended up with a geological record of architecture layers and there was never a business case to remove layers even though that was the intent of the new program when it started. The front end of the architecture changed the most over the past few decades. Some of the middle layer changed but not much changed on the back end because changes here can be so difficult and expensive to implement. The back end has seen new relational database systems rotated through and some clean-up work. Many Wealth Management firms would take issue with this point saying they have the best and newest throughout. The truth is quite different.

The robo-advisors do not have to use these architectures unless the Wealth Management firms force them to do so. Certainly, some Wealth Management firms will put their robo-advisor as part of their system engagement layer so that the financial advisor can use it to interact with the client. Wealth Management firms will not allow anyone to get between the financial advisor and the customer. This relationship is sacrosanct within a Wealth Management. The robo-advisors pure plays do not need large CRM systems and implement their own invasive ERP systems and they could use service bureaus for clearing and settlement.

What is the future for banking and wealth management? Figures 8.3 and 8.4 show new business models that are devoid of the financial accreted mess. The differences in the business models are this:

1. System of Engagement — this must support customers who are autonomous system.
2. Robo-Advisors — the performance of a robo-advisor, which can be deployed across all systems of engagements, will determine the success of a bank and wealth management firm in the future.

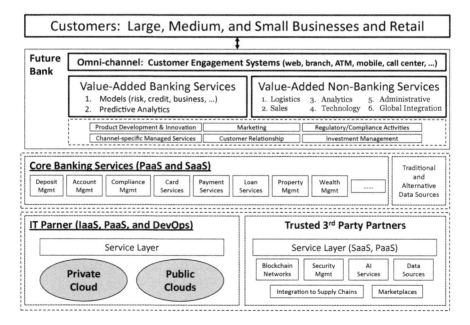

Figure 8.1: New business model for the bank business showing those areas that need to be automated.

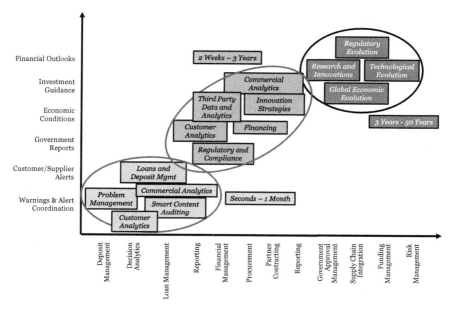

Figure 8.2: Data needed to automate the new banking business model.

The robo-advisors must be able to integrate with the rest of the business model.

3. Know Your Customer (KYC) — needs to use a blockchain to verify the identity of any customer even if that customer is an autonomous system.

4. Blockchain — processes to support a wide variety of blockchain networks that enable M2M transactions.

5. Crowdfunding Services — more and more the ability to support new and innovative ways to raise capital for personal and business loans, mortgages, and lines of credit will differentiate a bank and wealth management firm. It should enable autonomous system to contribute to this model.

A takeaway from these new models is that they have not changed much from the old models. This is because the regulatory frameworks in force are very prescriptive as to how banks operate, what they can do, and what they cannot do. The adoption of new technologies, however transformational, does not change current law.

The key is that it is possible for banks to automate much more of what they do if they so choose to do so. Arguments that this change is not justified by any business case can be powerful and are usually correct. However, start-ups in this field can start with an automation of many of these processes, especially if they take advantage of Value Creation Partners to perform specific tasks for them. A start-up can begin with the minimal number of Key Functions and Core and Enabling Functions as possible and execute them with multiple and integrated autonomous system. Over time, the start-up can bring the functions performed by Value Creation Partners in house to be done autonomously.

The question mark here is will regulators allow this level of automation to happen. As with all the other topics discussed in this book, the answer would be yes if (1) automation does not decrease the workload of a bureaucracy, and (2) the autonomous system themselves can be audited and regulated. This has been discussed above and will be discussed further below. The bottom-line is that regulatory bodies have grown over time and even with the advent of autonomous system, these bodies may find regulation easier and more pervasive.

3. Insurance and Changes to the Risk Pool

Start-ups in the insurance business typically make two mistakes: (1) forget about the fact that some entity needs to maintain the risk pool on their balance sheet (a multi-billion dollar entry), and (2) the prescriptive regulatory model imposed on this business from all 50 states and the Federal government. At one point, the average number of insurance-related bills introduced into the California state legislature reached a frequency of once a day. The infrastructure of humans and reporting capabilities is enormous and cost prohibitive for any start-up. This reporting can be outsourced but it is still a difficult and necessary component to any insurance business. Business analytics will allow risk to be more granular and better quantified. Disruption will be limited as no disruptor or start-up will want to take the insurance risk on their balance sheet. That will always be a role for the larger insurers. A widely accepted virtual currency might change this but the regulatory framework will preclude the use of virtual currencies for risk mitigation.

Figure. 8.3 shows a new business model for insurance companies whose business processes are largely automated. Much of the automation for insurance companies can be done via platforms. IoTs in cars and homes can be accessed to ascertain conditions and send data back to the AS. Claims services are largely automated today and can get to 80% or better automation now or in the near future. Product manufacturing will not benefit much from automation because each change to products or policies need approval by each of the 50 states and sometimes the federal government. The workflow for it can be automated. Much of the capabilities that enable insurance are available from existing platforms or those being developed.

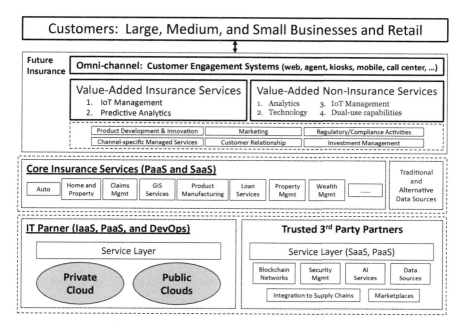

Figure 8.3: New business model for the insurance business showing those areas that need to be automated.

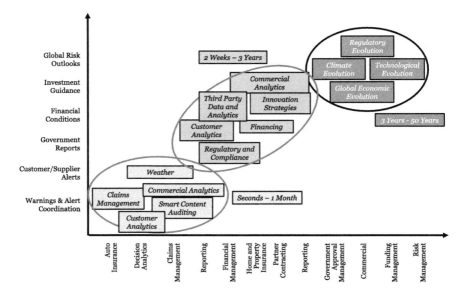

Figure 8.4: Data needed to automate the new insurance business model.

Figure 8.4 shows the data challenges for automated insurance companies. A key problem that property insurers have is that they do not have recent and actionable information on the homes and property they insure. One insurance company has to send people out around the country to visit homes that (1) have assessed values of greater than $800,000, (2) have paid premiums for at least 20 years, and (3) have never made a claim. In short, this insurance company does not know what it is insuring.

There is a solution to this problem; it has been and will continue to be a drone solution. The solution is to create a baseline description of all insured properties where this description has quantified attributes associated with the property. First and foremost is the roof and its attributes since the biggest problem for a property insurer is the roof. Roof attributes are roof size, shape, type, age, and any existing damage. Next are property attributes that are risk exposures. Examples of these are a pool, basketball net or court, or trees too close to the house. Other attributes present a tertiary risk to insurers such as distance to the nearest river, crime statistics, accidents in the general vicinity, and distance to the nearest fire hydrant and fire station.

It will soon be possible to overfly neighborhoods and capture the above information on every house using a drone and sensors. The major issue is policy and regulation and for the purposes of this example, we can assume that eventually the regulatory environment will allow this solution. The drones to do this work exist and there is a strong competency in operating them. The key to this solution are the sensors.

It is possible using the new small hyperspectral sensors to discriminate many of the property attributes and characterize them with one flyby.[b] Hyperspectral imagers take an image of an area in many different wavelengths simultaneously so that in one image cube, there would be hundreds of images of the area with each image at a different wavelength. The use of broadband filters can also be used to discriminate features but are less effective than hyperspectral sensors, which are effectively very narrow band filters.

The baseline is created by flying over neighborhoods and collecting hyperspectral data on all of the homes in the neighborhood. This data can then be analyzed so that all of the property attributes listed above can be measured. Man-made objects have certain reflectivity properties and it turns out that there is a difference in peak reflectivity between man-made and natural objects.[4,5] Hyperspectral data can be used to determine the size of a roof and its elevations to less than an inch accuracy without too much light contamination from natural objects like trees or leaves on the roof. The data also allows roof problems to be identified. The age of the roof can be estimated and even small hail dents are evident in images.

The hyperspectral images that are dominated by the reflected light of natural objects provide information on location, type, and condition of natural objects that are present on the property. It is possible to map out the centroid and extent of each tree, bush, garden, and other objects without contamination from man-made objects. Therefore, an autonomous drone can survey neighborhoods

---

[b] Hyperspectral imaging, https://en.wikipedia.org/wiki/Hyperspectral_imaging.

to quantify each property and properly assess the risk associated with insuring that property.

Insurance companies are also using IoTs to induce behavioral changes to their customers. Essentially the insurers are trying to improve the customer risk profile by encouraging specific changes to those insured activities like driving or owning a home or renting an apartment. Insurers are also examining how to insure other risks human have such as data and online financial risks.

How does an insurance business model change? As with the banks and wealth management firms, much of what they do is not under their control. The regulatory framework for insurers is even more prescriptive than banks. Therefore, many Core and Enabling Processes do not change and must still be present. The changes are the presence of blockchain services to be used in the sales and claims areas (discussed above), the inclusion of superior property data, both baseline and post-catastrophe, to help with pricing power and reduced expense ratios, and also crowdfunding services. The latter is a heretofore little explored area for insurers except in the reinsurance space.

Crowdfunding services could be another area of growth for insurance companies in that it allows for the risk pool to be more distributed and not on its balance sheet. This is a different take on the discussion of insurance start-ups above. It is possible (setting aside the time it would take for regulatory approval) for large insurance agencies to create a pool of wealthy clients to form their own insurance company and use the large insurers for regulatory compliance services, including reporting, and for reinsurance services. This has an appeal both to clients needing better returns on their wealth and insurers who can reduce their risks and expense ratios but not necessarily their revenues. It is also possible in this model for autonomous system to be a wealthy client who can contribute to the risk pool on behalf of their owners. There is no reason an autonomous system needs a human to tell it what is a good or bad risk; the ability of an autonomous system to figure that out for themselves is doable. It might also be possible for driverless cars, which are not owned by anyone, to also use their wealth to invest in this mechanism. Autonomous system might even be used to insure other autonomous system, possibly on very short timescales such as driving through a high-risk area. This all is enabled by one or more blockchains and autonomous system trained to operate in this space.

4. The Impact of Autonomous System to Financial Services

The world of financial services is already automated to a large extent and still has areas that can be significantly impacted by autonomous system. HFTs and other rote processing systems are currently in use and provide a level of service to customers that proves out the utility of an autonomous system in different financial domains. We see how the introduction of new technologies can have an impact but the depth and breadth of the impact will be throttled by prescriptive regulatory behavior and the banks themselves. Banks and other financial institutions are still highly manual and their incentives are not aligned to changing that anytime soon lest they compromise the significant income recognized with transaction fees. To maximize transaction fees, the number of transactions will always be maximized. The new technologies and autonomous system will be slowly stood up so as to control any changes, transformational or tactical, to ensure the trusted third party role does not disappear or be marginalized.

There is an opportunity for banks and wealth management firms to be blockchain pure plays and in that way start to become the dominant players in the field. Their capital requirements are such that a group of investors can provide working and reserve capitals. Robo-advisors can manage customers fully even if there is a need for a brick and mortar location where a customer can walk in for safe deposit services and be helped by a tele-robot or a robo-advisor who can move from device to device as the customer walks from the front door to the safe deposit boxes.

What about data needs? In Table 8.1, we list the types of data that autonomous system financial institutions will presumably need and what may or may not exist.

Table 8.1: Opportunities for big data in financial services.

	New Capabilities	As is Analysis	Management Horizon	Strategic Horizon
	System of Engagement	• Baby Boomer Behaviors • End user device management	• Millennial Behaviors • New end user device management (e.g., telepresence robots) • Customer personalization	• Post-Millennial Behaviors
Financial	Robo-Advisors	• Leverage existing providers • Integration into mobile devices	• Breadth and Depth • Enhancement of financial knowledge capital • Richer customer interactions	• Product Research • On-demand presence • Rich interactions with other autonomous system
Wealth Management				
Insurance	Blockchain Services	• Familiarization	• Pilot projects for use in basic processes and automation of internal manual processes	• Long-term monitoring by autonomous system of properties and humans • Transaction management
	Crowdfunding Services	• Familiarization	• Pilot programs to finance a certain class of loans (e.g., college) and insurance products	• Micro-insurance risk pools managed at the agent level • Maturation of process into portfolio management

There is a need to slowly transact into the use of these new capabilities because there is a natural resistance to further automation of the financial industry and the regulatory bodies, especially the growing aggressiveness of supranational bodies like the various European Union and its multiple regulatory bodies. The Systems of Engagements must learn how to deal with the generational changes that are occurring. Soon the Millennials will start to flex their financial muscles and they have been through a massive recession that seems to have colored their approach to finances. The use of robo-advisors will grow with time due to convenience and perception of better depth and breadth of knowledge it presents to the customer, especially the Millennials and Post-Millennials. These groups and to a certain extent Baby Boomers have been and will continue to increase their use of crowdfunding for a variety of uses.

One aspect is how will financial institutions work when their customers are autonomous system? There are possible modes where an autonomous system could accumulate wealth and be trained to use that wealth in altruistic or pure profit behaviors. Will financial institutions be allowed to have autonomous system as customers? What will regulatory bodies do to manage something they do not understand and do not want to deal with unless it meets their incentives (grow their organizations and regulate more).

References

1. Korn, M (6 May 2016) Imagine discovering that your teaching assistant really is a robot. *The Wall Street Journal.* http://www.wsj.com/articles/if-your-teacher-sounds-like-a-robot-you-might-be-on-to-something-1462546621

2. Russell, W (2013) *Winning with Risk Management (Financial Engineering and Risk Management — Volume 2)*, 1st Ed. Singapore: World Scientific.

3. Eule, A (2 April 2016). Robot advisors thrive. *Barrons.* http://www.barrons.com/articles/robo-advisors-thrive-1459570674.

4. Woolley, JT (1971). "Reflectance and transmittance of light by leaves", *Plant Physiol,* 47(5), 656–662. http://www.ncbi.nlm.nih.gov/pmc/articles/PMC396745/?page=4.

5. Parker, DS. *et al.* (2000). *Laboratory Testing of the Reflectance Properties of Roofing Materials.* Cocoa: Florida Solar Energy Center (FSEC), FSEC-CR-670-00, http://www.fsec.ucf.edu/en/publications/html/FSEC-CR-670-00/.

CHAPTER 9

Manufacturing

1. The Supply Chain As An Autonomous System

Manufacturing supply chains are the most complex, automated, and typically, best well-run of all supply chains. The two attributes of this supply chain that will eventually make then almost fully automated is (1) process standardization due to lean manufacturing and (2) a legacy of automation reaching back many decades. These two attributes, unique to manufacturing, will result in a faster evolution to supply chains that are more AS in nature. The lean manufacturing attribute has resulted in processes that are well-defined, repeatable, and measurable. In short, they are rote processes that are a perquisite to using AS. The legacy attribute will make AS adoption faster, easy, and less expensive than other industries discussed in this book.

Processes that are rote and have been for decades have a significant advantage over those that are not when deciding what processes to turn into an AS. The high quality data needed to create and maintain AS are present at multiple timescales (see Fig. 9.1). Process and data maturity have allowed and will continue to allow for processes to be turned into AS over the next decade.

The architecture of a manufacturing supply chain makes a few things clear. First the use of a private blockchain for a given product will be straightforward to implement (see Fig. 9.2). The value is to

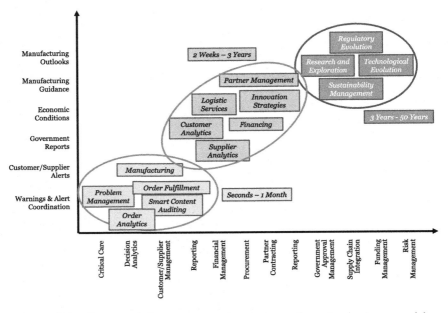

Figure 9.1: Data needed to automate the new manufacturing business model.

put all members of a supply chain onto the same blockchain. This will be a challenge because the blockchain will contract many smart contracts to govern the transactions. This will impact performance of supply chain transactions. In addition, the choice of a private blockchain for one supply chain has three key requirements to satisfy: (1) ensure the activity on the blockchain is visible to supply chain partners only; (2) establish and govern the controls over which transactions are permitted; and (3) enable mining to take place securely without proof of work.

Secondly, AS will make these supply chains agile, adaptable, and align supply chain partners. AS force a well-defined process definition and execution into a supply chain. If the data collected for the supply chain operation is correct, the training of the AI component will be optimal for supply chain operations. These pre-conditions will evolve processes that can handle short-term disruptions, react to changing market conditions, and ensure alignment amongst supply chain partners.

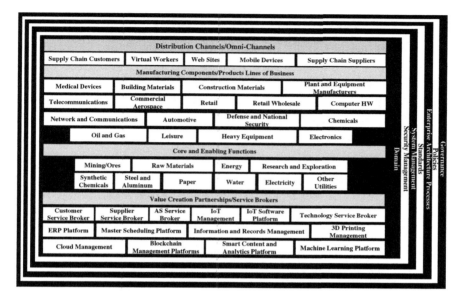

Figure 9.2: New business model for the manufacturing business showing those areas that need to be automated.

Finally, it appears that the use of 3D printing, even at the level of a human in their garage, will enhance the quality and cost of a supply chain. 3D printing would allow a customer to source parts from thousands of vendors and not just a few. It may take many dozens of vendors to provide the requisite number of parts. The management of these vendors is simplified when the automation is done using the cloud and each 3D printer is viewed as an IoT. The printed part is just data.

The reason platform companies are pushing the IoT platform is that they want to capture the high quality data traditionally present in companies that use their products. Companies have created high quality data over the past decades and that data has not been available to the platform companies. This has changed in the past decade as cars have become so complicated that only a manufacturer or its proxy can access the data to do the repair and maintenance work (when was the last time you changed your spark plugs?). The downside to this dynamic is that companies are losing access to the data they need to innovate and grow.

2. It Is All About the Robot — Almost

Robots were made for the manufacturing supply chain. Companies that import raw materials such as iron ore and raw minerals turn these into rolled steel and other products that are then used for manufacturing finished products such as car parts, machine parts, aircraft parts, and construction materials. These are accomplished by rote processes around mining, logistics, manufacturing, and distribution. Companies are recognizing that removing the human element from these processes has significant benefits besides cost reduction. Safety is a close second for the automation argument, followed by quality of the product produced due to manufacturing consistency done without interruption. It is clear that the trend is toward fulling autonomous supply chains for manufacturing but there will always be humans in the loop. In fact, what is being seen during this transformation is that the types of jobs being created required data scientist skills such as programming, data mining, and analytics.

Driverless cars are viewed with much curiosity but not much has been done in the way of understanding the impact these will have when deployed in large numbers. There is one area where 3D printing when coupled with autonomous system could have a significant impact. Our research shows that the entire automotive supply chain can be disrupted to such an extent that layoffs and tax bases will be significantly disadvantaged. The need for more cars is reduced. The need for expensive repairs can be mitigated by someone in a garage with a printer. Cars might not be owned but a subscription fee paid that allows a human or another autonomous system to request a car or truck via an app on-demand. The prospects for the automotive supply chain is bleak and is another area where the government may decide to throttle back on the use of the new technologies to prevent the downside of transformational change from happening.

3. Autonomous Mining

A leading indicator for autonomous operations are mining operations where the process of going from the mine to the port to ship the raw materials is mostly autonomous.[1] Mining is one of the most hazardous jobs in any country and the cost of using humans and ensuring their safety has a significant cost to it. It is an area to address and it appears that automation of this major process is doable and leading companies in the industry are pursuing automation of their mining operations and the transport of these raw materials to ports. Joy Global is a US company who has provided equipment for mining since 1919 and a perusal of its website shows the products used to automate the entire surface mining and below ground mining activities.

Rio Tinto has invested time and money to automate the open pit mines in Australia and create automated mining in general. Its Mine of the Future™ program originated because many of its mining operations in Australia require humans to be transported in to the mines to do the work and for engineers to drive the trains with the iron ore long distances. According Rio Tinto, its Mine of the Future™ program "is creating next-generation systems and technologies to drive Rio Tinto to become a global leader in fully integrated, automated mining".[a] Rio Tinto has deployed driver trucks at its mines that have currently covered almost 5 million km moving mined materials from the mine egress to the transportation hubs. Rio Tinto is piloting a driverless train to deliver iron ore across Australia. The autonomous locomotives will run on the 1500 km rail network that links the Rio iron mines in the Pilbara region of Western Australia with the ports of Cape Lambert and Dampier. Rio has invested $518 million to build out the heavy haul railroad which is behind schedule in April 2016. Regardless of timing, this effort shows that the production process can be coupled with the logistics process to complete an autonomous system for a key part of any supply chain.

Another leading indicator that autonomous system are becoming operational here is that while jobs at the mines have decreased, there is a need for employees to manage autonomous operations. These new jobs require analytical skills that are just being taught at universities. Rio Tinto finds itself hiring people to do jobs similar to drone pilots to ensure trucks and trains operate properly. While it is true

---

[a] Rio Tinto Mine of the Future™, Next-generation mining: People and technology working together, http://www.riotinto.com/documents/Mine_of_The_Future_Brochure.pdf

that the autonomous system systems being used can continue to learn how to execute these processes better and better, it is not clear that this learning is being done on timescales to completely eliminate up to 95% or more humans from the mining operations. We have no evidence that suggest that a key process like mining operations can be 100% autonomous with no human intervention. The latter will slowly decrease with time but for the foreseeable future while the autonomous system support for mission critical processes are matured, it should be expected that jobs will still exist and that the nature of the jobs will be different and need to be staffed by people who can be flexible with their job descriptions. This small example provides insights into the future of jobs.

4. Automated Ports

The next step in the manufacturing process is to get the raw materials from its export location to its import location. The US imported $2.19T of goods in 2014.[b] This includes computers, broadcast equipment, crude petroleum, parts for cars, trucks and aircraft, clothing, packaged medicaments, gold, silver, and 19 mineral commodities for which there are little or no domestic sources: arsenic, asbestos, bauxite, cesium, fluorspar, gallium, natural graphite, indium, manganese, natural sheet mica, niobium, industrial quartz crystal, rubidium, scandium, strontium, tantalum, thallium, thorium, and vanadium.[c] This $2.19T of goods comes into ports on the West Coast, East Coast, and the Gulf States. The Port of Long Beach, the second largest in the United States handled 7.2 million containers in 2015 with over half being imports such as crude oil, electronics, plastics, furniture, and clothing. The work to load and unload ships has been a highly manual and automation

---

[b] OEC (2014), What does the United States import? (2014), http://atlas.media.mit.edu/en/visualize/tree_map/hs92/import/usa/all/show/2014/

[c] AGI (2016), Which mineral commodities used in the United States need to be imported?, http://www.americangeosciences.org/critical-issues/faq/which-mineral-commodities-used-united-states-need-be-imported

has come slow to this part of the supply chain for two reasons: (1) unions resisting the onset of automation and (2) the cost to automate a port.

Manufacturing has institutionalized the use of intermodal transport with containers that can be loaded on ships in Southeast Asia arrive at its location in Des Moines, IA, without opening the container. The process has become so rote that the ports themselves are being automated so that containers can be loaded from trains or trucks onto container ships, delivered to another port where robots remove the containers off the ships, and load them onto trains and trucks for delivery.[2,3] It is estimated that the productivity of a port that adopts automation technology will increase by 30%. The Port of Long Beach has just opened up an automated terminal that cost them over $1 billion to construct. It is expected this terminal will service about half of the port traffic including the new supercontainer ships that are starting to show up at US ports. The typical complications that arise with this automation are more about the loss of jobs at the ports than the technology. Economics is driving the transformation of ports to be fully autonomous meaning that humans are needed for overseeing operations and for performing the loading/unloading tasks for which robots are not yet capable of accomplishing with any degree of certainty. And this is not just a US dynamic. The Port of Rotterdam has undergone an almost complete autonomous operational makeover and has recognized the benefits of this automation investment.

The next step in the process is to allow for autonomous trucks to deliver and receive the containers from transportation hubs where the containers are moved to other trucks, trones, and trains. This process is discussed in greater details in the Logistics chapter. The success to date of the Rio Tinto trains provides the justification that driverless trucks and long-haul trains can be used in the United States and elsewhere. Their operations can provide the data such as cost, time, and roles to be used in estimating the implementation of fully autonomous operations. Rio Tinto can also provide insights on how the job descriptions will change and what kinds of new jobs will emerge in the next few decades.

5. Autonomous Factories and the 80/20 Rule

The use of automation in factories has been a well-known phenomenon and is now starting to accelerate. At this point, there are about 66 autonomous system (autonomous system with actuators, i.e., robots) per 10,000 workers averaged globally. This represents a huge opportunity as Japan has 1,520 autonomous system per 10,000 workers. It is expected that the 10% of all manufacturing tasks that are done now by autonomous system will grow to 45% of manufacturing tasks within 10 years. Boeing made 564 planes a year or 217 workers per plane in 1998. Boeing made 760 planes in 2015 using about 109 workers per plane, and the figure is falling. China, the largest producer of industrial robots, intends to start replacing millions of workers with autonomous system of varying degree of complexity. China, the United States, Japan, South Korea, and Germany currently account for 70% of the global market. Japan has the largest installed base of industrial robots, accounting for 20% of the global total. The Foxconn Technology Group which makes iPhones stated that they will replace up to 70% of their workers with autonomous system but then walked back those comments and seemed to have settled on a plan that in 5 years, the autonomous system will take over 30% of the manpower.[4] Overall, it appears that autonomous system makes sense when the cost of an autonomous system represents a 15% discount over the cost of a worker for those industries where the worker role is rote.[5]

A detailed literature search and analysis shows that at this time, this 15% discount appears to be a good number though our research indicates that it is more like 20–25% for complex tasks. It is believed this is due to the fact that as autonomous system do more complex tasks, it takes time for the quality of work to achieve that commensurate with a human and then exceed it. Also, people who perform complex tasks tend to be compensated greater than those who are just performing rote tasks. Performance of autonomous systems is expected to improve by 5% each year so if that is the case, in 10 years autonomous system should be at least 65% better than they are today though that appears to be a lower limit given the tendency for technology evolution to accelerate with time.

Another research outcome that is still being pursued is how European countries are starting to ramp up the use of autonomous system as well. Within a decade there could be competitive manufacturing capabilities in countries heretofore uncompetitive for large-scale manufacturing in the same manner that China and Korea are today and the United States is trending back into at this point. The countries investing in autonomous system manufacturing are Italy, France, the Czech Republic, Poland, and Turkey. The remaining countries such as Spain, England, Belgium, Netherlands, and Sweden are ramping down investments in autonomous system. Will Italy, France, the Czech Republic, Poland, and Turkey start to become centers of manufacturing? Existing labor laws and labor organizations will seek to slow any transition to significant autonomous system footprint but the fact that Germany and France are investing heavily bodes well that a gradual replacement of workers will occur, leading to reduced costs, greater factory productivity, and presumably higher quality products and services.

Another research area being monitored is the use of autonomous system in Africa. The value proposition in Africa has always been that labor is cheap as long as the local environment has good governance. South Africa does have some autonomous system factories but there is no great presence there or anywhere else. The natural resources of Africa and the rate and approach its population takes in adoption of new technologies lead one to believe that autonomous system could do very well there, taking advantage of an innovative society able to internalize new technologies. The key to any improvement to Africa is good governance and the Ibrahim Index of African Governance is an annual report card that measures the governance of African governments in such a way that they can be compared to the developed world. The latest report[d] shows a continent in which progress in governance is stalling. The index itself, which takes into account a variety of indicators ranging from corruption and rule of law to infrastructure and

---

[d]Mo Ibrahim Foundation, IIAG Data Portal, http://mo.ibrahim.foundation/iiag/data-portal/

sanitation shows change much lower than expected based on the average from 2011. Previous years the index had shown steady improvements by most countries. More worrying are signs of reversal at the top of the list. The ten countries that ranked best have changed to such an extent that five have seen a decline in their governance scores since 2011. The main reasons for the stall are declines in those relating to safety and the economy. The average decline in measures of safety and the rule of law is reduced by conflicts in South Sudan, Libya, and the Central African Republic. Mauritius, Botswana, and Tanzania have also fallen even though they are relatively peaceful.

The automation of the manufacturing supply chain will be complete when the end point of the supply chain, that is the autonomous system factories, are able to integrate with the rest of the supply chain, from mine or field, to autonomous system factory. Countries that are investing in autonomous system manufacturing should see their manufacturing cost competitiveness improve when compared with the rest of the world. Nations such as those listed above and Austria, Brazil, and Russia that are not investing in autonomous system manufacturing should see their relative cost competitiveness erode and start to fall behind. This dynamic is because countries that are not investing in autonomous system manufacturing tend not to invest in those integration points such as autonomous ports and autonomous transportation hubs (one exception is Rotterdam, The Netherlands). The danger is that these countries that start to fall behind if they cannot support the autonomous operations that will eventually be required by the back end of the manufacturing supply chain. Africa is in danger of being disadvantaged here as well as it has few Panamax-class ports, which are required for establishing autonomous ports.

6. "Dad, What Was a Car Dealership?"

There is one area where 3D printing when coupled with autonomous system could have a significant impact. We describe the future and then how our world might transact into that future.

The future is this. Every morning when I wake up there is a car in my driveway to take me to work. I get in and using my smartphone app, I give the address of my work to the car, sit back, and maybe fall asleep again. The car delivers me to work. After work, I use the same app to request a ride home. A different car shows up and drives me home though if I want to make a few stops along the way I can. On Friday afternoon, the car that picks me up at work is actually a big SUV. I get home early and the family packs the car for the weekend at the lake. Off we go to the lake, doing whatever we want to do during the drive and a few hours later we are at the lake house. On Sunday night, we arrive home, unpack, and the SUV leaves. We use our app to order food for the morning and when we wake up Monday morning, there is a container with the food we ordered sitting in our driveway. An hour later, a car arrives to take me to work. A second car arrives to take the kids to school because my wife is not feeling well and cannot drive the kids. A third car comes to take her to the hospital and it is equipped with the ability to monitor her vital signs and store it on her medical blockchain on her flash drive.

We do not own or lease a car. We have an agreement with a rental company for $149/month for the use of two cars per day of a certain class or one car of a larger class. We can if we want specify the color of the car and other attributes. We can specify that there are certain cars we do not want or, given the ease that a government can monitor autonomous system, we might not be allowed certain cars because our carbon footprint for the month is out of credits and we have to do all electrical cars or no cars at all.

The above scenario is a favorite one of driverless car enthusiasts and smartphone app developers. Everyone likes to discuss things like this without thinking through all the implications. The implications are significant. Our research into these implications is concerning to car dealerships, car manufacturers, and the entire automotive supply chain. Our results are summarized in Table 9.1.

Table 9.1 shows our current estimate to the automotive supply chain assuming that driverless cars become the norm, that car parts can be printed by anyone with enough money to buy a printer and

Table 9.1: Estimate of impact of on-demand printed cars.

	Present	Near Future	Far Future
Number of cars sold	7,740,912	5,750,000	1,000,000
Total number of cars produced	4,250,000	3,500,000	750,000
Number of cars and trucks on the road	253,000,000	200,000,000	75,000,000
Driverless cars on the road	10	1,000,000+	50,000,000
Total number of employees in auto supply chain	866,000	500,000	50,000
Total number of car dealerships in the United States	17,838	16,000	<5,000

use it, and that people eschew car ownership in favor of renting what they need when they need it. The results indicate:

1. A large reduction in the employees in the automotive supply chain
2. An 85% reduction in the number of cars sold
3. An 80%–85% reduction in the number of cars produced
4. A 70% reduction of cars and trucks on the road (this also assumes the reduction of trucks based on the discussion above on logistics)
5. A massive increase in the number of driverless cars
6. A 70% or higher reduction in the number of dealerships in the United States

The model that determined Table 9.1 is predicated on the scenario presented above. This exercise was meant to estimate an impact if everyone used an on-demand model for their transportation needs. This is not an effort to predict the future and start using it to make decisions. This exercise shows that the use of autonomous system modes of transportation will have a significant, yes even gut-wrenching, impact.

We wanted to address the "robots will put everyone out of work" commentary. The love of cars and great skills sets in the automotive industry cannot mean that all those people will cease working. There is a very good possibility that these people might become the new automotive manufacturers in their own right. We can expand on the above scenario to explain this and why the loss of jobs in Table 9.1 does not mean that many people are out of work; it means they have in large part repurposed themselves.

Who owns those cars that show up every day to drive me to work? The car company? The dealership? The rental car company? A group of investors? No one? Or does the car own itself (and how did it come to own itself?)? The car is an autonomous system and can determine what passengers it can service based on location, bid price, and maximizing profitability (do I sit at the airport or do I service several fares during the day?). Several ownership and maintenance models work:

1. Humans lease/owns the car that the dealership printed for them and has a dealership maintain the car.
2. Dealership owns the car that it printed and assembled and maintains it. Car is on-demand.
3. Group of investors owns the cars, derives a return from its on-demand service model, and has the dealership maintain it.
4. A rental car company leases the cars from a group of investors and provides the on-demand service and other value-added services to the passengers (the airline model).
5. The government or a NGO pays for driverless cars to be built and let them operate themselves for the benefit of society. The car pays the dealership to maintain it based on revenues from passengers.
6. The car owns itself. Everything the car needs to do it can do online (create its own LLC, get a bank account, find customers, take payments, pay for gas and repairs, pay taxes, etc.) and all its profits are available for taxing authorities or other community uses.

It is necessary to expand on the definition of "dealership." A dealership can be what we think of it today or it could be several former automotive supply chain workers who have multiple 3D printers and can build and maintain vehicles.

Table 9.2: Opportunities for analytics in manufacturing.

New Capabilities	As Is Analysis	Management Horizon	Strategic Horizon
System of Engagement	• Pilot M2M Transactions	• New end user device management (e.g., telepresence robots) • Operationalize M2M Transactions using blockchain	• Fully Autonomous
Mining Ports Factories Automotive Supply Chain Robo-Advisors	• Pilot Support and MRO support	• Customer personalization • Breadth and Depth Enhancement of manufacturing knowledge capital • Richer customer interactions	• Product Research • On-demand presence • Rich interactions with other autonomous system
Blockchain Services	• Familiarization	• Pilot projects for use in basic processes and automation of internal manual processes	• Long-term monitoring by autonomous system of properties and humans • Transaction management

7. The Impact of Autonomous Manufacturing

Will manufacturing provide the first completely autonomous supply chain? Or does "completely" mean a supply chain with humans located in a control center that oversee supply operations? [T] Automation and robots have been a staple of manufacturing for many years. We address the ability of these supply chains to be automated from beginning to end, even those areas like mining and transportation of bulk material. This supply chain should rival the food supply chain in which one reaches Level 4 first and which one is mostly Level 4 in all processes. A key enabler to supply chain automation is M2M transactions that use the blockchain for product tracing and perhaps reward one another with Bitcoins or other virtual currency. The 3D printer has the ability to completely disrupt manufacturing allowing autonomous systems to define their own supply chains that can be dynamic in nature and changed to fit any purpose on any timescale (Table 9.2).

References

1. Diss, K (28 October 2015). Driverless trucks move all iron ore at Rio Tinto's Pilbara mines, in world first. *ABC News*. http://www.abc.net.au/news/2015-10-18/rio-tinto-opens-worlds-first-automated-mine/6863814

2. Phillips, EE (28 March 2016). Supersize ships prompt more automation at ports. The Wall Street Journal. http://www.wsj.com/articles/supersize-ships-prompt-more-automation-at-ports-1459202549

3. Phillips, EE (27 March 2016). Massive robots keep docks shipshape. The Wall Street Journal. http://www.wsj.com/articles/massive-robots-keep-docks-shipshape-1459104327

4. Kan, M (26 June 2015). Foxconn's CEO backpedals on robot takeover at factories. *IDG News Service in Computer World*. http://www.computerworld.com/article/2941272/emerging-technology/foxconns-ceo-backpedals-on-robot-takeover-at-factories.html

5. Boston Consulting Group (10 February 2015). Takeoff in robotics will power the next productivity surge in manufacturing. http://www.bcg.com/d/press/10feb2015-robotics-power-productivity-surge-manufacturing-838

CHAPTER 10

Healthcare

1. Introduction

Why will healthcare be automated? The answer to that is simple. The doubling of medical knowledge, that is the amount of time it takes for the amount of known medical information to double in size will be 73 days by 2020. In 1950, the doubling times was 50 years. IN 1908 it was 7 years and in 2010 it was 3.5 years. The minimum length of training for a doctor is about 7 years so students will experience multiple doublings of knowledge from which they will have to apply that knowledge to the medical problems. And will patients expect anything less?

The author had surgery on his left knee 25 years apart. The first was to remove torn cartilage in 1986 and the second was a knee replacement in 2014. The experiences were vastly different and provides an example to consider how autonomous systems will impact healthcare. The key takeaway was the significant difference in the processes executed from when the patient walked in the door to when they were discharged. The differences represent the evolution that has occurred in healthcare over the past three decades. These differences are not just new technologies and surgical procedures; these differences are also the processes executed to run a hospital, the creation of satellite critical care centers, the stronger integration of university-based research center development and the retail hospital, and the development of facilities optimized for certain procedures whose numbers have grown dramatically as the baby boomer generation has aged.

The aforementioned patient had his torn cartilage removed in a general hospital. The admissions process was similar for this procedure as it was for other procedures. The reasons for being admitted had to be explained multiple times to multiple people as the patient moved from office to office that was part of the admitting process. There was no identification verification during the process and no validation of the exact procedure to be done. The journey from admitting offices to the operating room consisted of being moved from admitting to a room where nothing happened, then to another room where nothing happened, and then to a bed where the patient had to get into a hospital gown. The patient was then wheeled to another temporary location where the IV hookups began and a nurse finally appeared (for the first time) to discuss the procedure. The nurse had about 10 pounds of documents on a clipboard and did not ask for identification or validation of the reasons why the patient was there. It was then that a wristband with the name of the patient was installed. From this location the patient was wheeled into the operating room where they had the presence of mind to ask the people there if they were expecting someone to remove the cartilage on his left knee. He refused the anesthesiologist's commands until the surgeon came in to verify what was being done as the patient had never been allowed to meet the surgeon prior to the operation. The discharge process has fewer steps to it but took several hours to complete including a 30-minute wait in a wheelchair waiting for someone to wheel them out of the hospital to go home.

Contrast that with the knee replacement process. The patient received a booklet that had the exact process described and a checklist of all the steps along with the names of the people who would be seen, the location, the reason for seeing them, and at what times the patient would see them. The patient arrived at the front desk of the facility that services only hip and knee replacement patients at the time requested. The process described in the booklet was executed as described, everyone who came into contact with the patient examined the wristband (the first thing the patient was asked to put on), validated the procedure being done, and who was doing it. The final two people met were the anesthesiologist and the surgeon. Upon entering the operating room, both were there to greet the patient. For the 3 days of recovery, the patient knew who would be coming into the room and why. This included the physical therapists, nurses, pain coordinator (very helpful in fact!), and other people whose roles were nontraditional but clearly there because they enhanced the recovery process. There was even an IT person who supported the patient for needs on wireless connectivity, cable TV, and the other electronic capabilities in the room.

These two processes represent a best practice for their day and it is clear that process improvements occurred along with technical breakthroughs and amazing new surgical procedures. They also represent a standardization of the process of healthcare for certain procedures. The latter example is for patients whose procedures are done many times per week with little variation. Hospitals have learned that standardizing common procedures is a best practice from many other fields such as manufacturing and retail. The patient watched the technology involved and there clearly were some workflow system in place that drove all aspects of the work. It is clear that many parts of this procedure process could be automated as the process is rote and is supported by common IT components such as what one would find on a factory floor. The one difference is that it is not possible to replace the humans in this process to any great degree because the state of robotics is weak in creating robots that can move and function as a nurse, physical therapist, or pain coordinator. We discuss later the opportunities for a robot to replace a surgeon or anesthesiologist while currently there has been progress with surgeons using a robotic extension of themselves to do the work.

This standardization is not possible when a patient comes in with symptoms but no identification of an underlying cause. Think of an emergency room. A step not done in the above process was the diagnostic step. Can this step be automated similar to what happens in science fiction where all the patient has to do is stand there while the doctor runs a wand over them or a bed they lay on that instantly diagnoses everything? And what about an ER situation where the patient is a gunshot victim. Can the process to save that life be automated? An autonomous system that can perform accurate diagnosis rapidly, more rapid than the degradation rate of the medical condition, will impact healthcare more than standardization of knee replacement procedures.

The best and first use of AS in healthcare will be in decision support systems (DSS), i.e., systems that improve patient outcomes (see Fig. 10.1). The business capabilities for DSS are most similar to the DSS capabilities being used now in other industries like financial services and supply chains. This will be challenging given the data timescales in healthcare. The differences and gaps (see Fig. 10.2) are more acute here than in other industries. The data needed to train an ER need data from different timescales and from different domains. How would the DSS know that a stomach issue in an ER patient brought into Cook County Hospital in Chicago at Saturday at 2AM

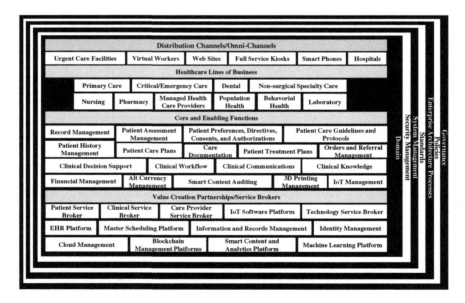

Figure 10.1: New business model for the healthcare business showing those areas that need to be automated.

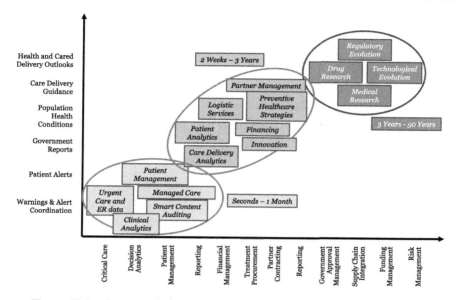

Figure 10.2: Data needed to automate the new healthcare business model.

is probably a gunshot wound while at Good Shepherd Hospital Barrington IL, 40 miles away, it is food poisoning? The former requires crime data and almost real time information while the latter is something determined by multi-year trends.

The most probable next use of AS in healthcare will be diagnostics and chronic condition monitoring that can use IoTs. The use of IoTs such as wrist devices, eyeglasses, and implants will be key for practitioners to monitor patients and take the sort of pre-emptive action normally reserved for machines maintenance.

Farther in the future, expect improvements with patient engagement, research, and chronic care management. Patient engagement has intriguing possibilities for a rich interaction with avatars. Patients can interact with a doctor's avatar and vice versa.

An adjacent use of AS for the healthcare system is real-time cyber security AS. Medical businesses are notoriously poor with the maturity of the cybersecurity practices. They will be sitting targets for future cyberattacks especially those carried out by an AS created by an adversary for just this purpose. The medical businesses will need to turn to a platform approach to strengthening their defenses and ability to continue as a business when confronted with this issue.

2. Automating Diagnosis — Where Humans and Autonomous Systems Work Together Best

There is a significant body of research directed toward replacing the doctor with an AI. A literature review uncovered a common theme among this work in that it is assumed that as a human walks into an exam room and is confronted by an AI that the AI will start at ground zero to determine what the problem with the human is. The AI would start with the symptoms of headache, sore throat, and listlessness and then start to examine every possible disease that could cause these symptoms. It may or may not take account of the fact that the human is a child. A human, not even a doctor but a well-informed parent, would look at the person, look for evidence of white dots in the throat, and deduce strep throat contracted at school once seeing the white dots. This simple example demonstrates what most efforts in autonomous diagnosis have concluded: rapid diagnosis, that is diagnosis on timescales shorter than the progression of the medical condition is best served through a judicious use of human and autonomous system. Over time as an autonomous system is used by the human to diagnose conditions, the autonomous system will learn the idiosyncrasies of diagnosis. This learning could take decades to converge to a learning solution that would allow for the human to be marginalized.

A frustrating part of figuring out what is wrong with a person is the process of diagnosing the underlying cause. A nurse or doctor in an emergency room situation may only have seconds to minutes to determine the problem a patient is facing. Would they know the person with the gunshot wound in their left shoulder is a drug mule who digested a package of drugs? If the package is punctured the gunshot wound will be the least of the patient's worries. How quickly can a team in the emergency room converge to a correct diagnosis?

The autonomous system for healthcare is best described not as we have been as a three-legged stool: IoTs, analytics, and autonomous system. For healthcare diagnosis, we change autonomous system to autonomous system + Human. This is a recognition that while we know much about the human body, it is necessary to blend the ability to recall vast amounts of relevant information that a doctor or nurse cannot possibly do with the bedside manner, gut intuition, and sixth senses that it is impossible to impart to an autonomous system. A doctor or nurse cannot store thousands of journal articles on hundreds of conditions but they can spot a drug mule quickly. Try codifying the ability to recognize a criminal into a set of rules for an autonomous system to execute. What about a diagnosis process that occurs in a doctor office where the patient starts off with headaches, nausea, constipation, and feeling lethargic. Is this because they have a brain tumor or are on the Atkins low carbohydrate diet?

Various diagnoses occur at different timescales. ER diagnoses have seconds to minutes to get it right. A doctor can be more contemplative and take hours to days. Psychologists might take months to years to determine if a person is bipolar. This implies that the autonomous system to support the humans is not the same for the diagnosis process when the process occurs on different timescales. The ER autonomous system might use different algorithms to do the classification of problems rather than some more sophisticated algorithm that might be more granular but take more time to execute. The autonomous system should know that certain problems arrive at the ER at certain times of the day and day of the week. Therefore, the diagnostic process needs to have a time dependency to it as well as a different prioritization of what to look for in a patient. The autonomous system should know to look for gunshot wounds around the body for a 20-year-old patient who is bleeding and is brought in on a Saturday night. The autonomous system should know that a child brought in before school might have things like strep throat or brought in during or after school might have some playground injury. The diagnostic process is not a single process; it is a catch-all term for many different types of processes and the autonomous system that supports each will have differences. It would help if when a patient arrives at an ER or doctor office that the Observe phase is minimal so that more time can be spent with ascertaining underlying causes.

When people takes their car to be emission tested, the testing facility simply plugs a computer into a port in the car underneath the steering wheel. A few minutes later, the computer can pronounce pass or fail based on the data it has downloaded from the car. The data on the car stays with the car. The technician does not have to search various sources of data to put together a complete picture of the car at that point in time. However, the car does not keep its history, only data on its current state. This is one drawback to cars today. Nowhere is the history of the car kept in one spot. It is spread across dealerships and repair shops in the form of printed reports. Is this pattern useful for healthcare?

Is it possible for a human to carry with them their entire medical history that can be accessed by any medical provider at any time with the permission of the human? Of course. Keeping in mind that the state of healthcare IT is consistently 15 years behind the leading edge of IT like financial services and setting aside the regulatory/privacy issues, let's assume that a human had with them their entire medical history from birth to present time including X-ray images, CAT scans, MRIs ultrasounds, EKGs, EEGs, medication history, blood test results, daily blood pressure readings, and the many occurrences of common ailments like the flu. This is less data than it might seem. One of the authors estimated that all his data from knee surgery back to birth could fit on an existing 100 GB flash drive. This data set while small is extremely valuable, so it qualifies as analytics based on its value alone. The memory device capable of wireless connectivity could be used by any medical personal to ascertain problems and symptoms within seconds once medical devices connected with the device via Bluetooth or wireless connection. Exploitation of the data when enriched with the vast stores of medical knowledge could be done in a short period of time and whether in an ER, doctor's office, or a psychologist's office, analytics could be produced and visualized for medical personnel to see what could possibly be the underlying cause. The complex and error-prone diagnostic process could be automated to the point where the medical experts can start at a better point in the diagnostic process rather than always starting at the beginning.

The collection and processing parts of this can be done automatically given the work being done by medical device start-ups and data mining start-ups that currently exist. Sensors exist that can continually take readings of the many attributes of the human body. These sensors can be internal or external to the body. For example, a network of sensors can be worn underneath a shirt or blouse to take readings and communicate with implanted devices. There could even be a master node on the body that is cloud-enabled to store data and do further analysis on the condition of the human to provide them with simple analysis of their conditions.

It is generally believed that healthcare would benefit from the use of the blockchain. The bcEHR is generating a lot of interest and differing opinions on how to use it. First and foremost, the blockchain can address the trust and verification issue in medical records. One of the problems that healthcare stakeholders have with electronic medical records they do not own or manage is whether the record is complete and has not been tampered with by some entity who has not recorded those changes. This is not some idle concern. Anthem had 80 million patient and employee records accessed by outside hackers[1] and UCLA Health had 4.5 million patient records breached from the outside.[2] There has also been reports of hospitals experiencing ransomware with regard to patient records. A doctor or hospital would not know if a breach did more than steal information on patients. Hackers can also insert information into electronic medical records and given that they may not be trained in the medical arts, inserting what they believe to be innocuous information (patient has a peanut allergy) might prevent life-saving drugs being given to the patient if the drug had serious side effects for those who do have peanut allergies.

The completeness of a medical record is even more difficult to validate and missing diagnosis or injuries could also lead to problems with future activities performed on the patient. There is no way that a person over 50 can remember all of the places they received medical care and what that care entailed. A person getting a knee replacement will not remember the dozen of ways their knee was hurt, when, in what circumstances, and what the X-rays taken after some injuries, showed. Throw in a few CAT scans or MRIs and who knows all of the injuries sustained did over time to a knee. And it is not just the ultimate diagnosis that could be missing. The symptoms experienced are typically discussed but sometimes not memorialized in a way that can be stored for future use. One study found that patients will list more symptoms than those symptoms that show up on a nurse or doctor notes.[3] Nurses and doctors typically make on-the-spot assessments of whether a symptom will have relevancy and this arises from the experiences in dealing with patients in the past. However, it is also to do with being tired and not fully realizing what the patient is saying.

The bcEHR could work with no centralization of authority or provenance for each patient record. Each visit to a healthcare provider would result in that provider adding to the patient bcEHR and this additive information could be annotated and verified by the blockchain. The next visit of the patient to the same or different healthcare provider could use the blockchain to verify that nothing had been tampered with in the bcEHR and the doctor can be assured that the information is complete and accurate.

The patient does not have to carry all of their bcEHR with them but could carry key parts of it and the permission to access the rest of it that is stored persistently in the cloud. There are two areas that would benefit immediately from this scenario when combined with IoT. The first are for humans who find themselves in catastrophic situations like earthquakes or hurricanes. The efficiencies of the first responders would be enhanced if they could immediately ascertain the condition of the injured human upon arrival. The connection to the human would be immediate and decisions could be made in a fraction of the time that it would take now. In fact with wireless connectivity, a triage unit could identify all injured parties within a 10 mile radius and know the conditions of the humans and know where to direct medical personnel to treat the most severely injured rather than the search and rescue that is done now.

The second area would be for the military and there are two possibilities here. The first is for commanders to monitor their troops in battle to determine the current state of physical conditions. Are they tired, dehydrating without knowing it, or stressed to the point where they need to be told to stand down for a few minutes. Additionally when the soldier is injured and being transported to the triage or hospital, sensors could continually provide updates to in situ medical personnel with the bcEHR of the soldier continually updated. This information could then be provided to the medical staff at their destination who could rapidly see what occurred to the soldier and what was done en route. The medical staff could monitor this in real time and know what problems were inbound and prepare.

The information captured on a soldier in real time has additional value to those other than the medical staff preparing to save the soldier's life. The information contained in the soldier bcEHR could be passed on to the military supply chain. This organization would aggregate the information received from other injured soldiers and have precise information on who was hurt and the extent of the injuries. The supply organization would also know that a particular medical unit needed specific items that could be sent to the unit without request. Raw materials for the 3D printers to create pieces of organs or prosthetic items might need resupply in addition to drugs and blood.

The key points of this section are that (1) the healthcare autonomous system is really a human plus and autonomous system and (2) access to a patient bcEHR is important to servicing a patient. The human and autonomous system both need one another to effectively diagnose a patient, assuming they have a fairly complete record of a patient that is trustworthy and complete. The diagnosis process can have many characteristic timescales depending on the context within which the examination is done and the manner in which information on the patient is combined in different contexts can have value for short-term diagnosis or possibly long-term trends.

3. The Healthcare Companion

The Japanese are at the forefront of creating robots to be companions of the elderly.[4] Across the globe the world is expected to need more healthcare workers than there are now and the need is especially acute for home healthcare. The percentage of the US population aged 65 or older is currently at 13%, but that number is expected to nearly double by 2050.[5] There are a number of tasks a home healthcare robot could perform. Companionship is an obvious one. A robot able to converse with a person would quickly become a friend in every sense of the word. The robot would be at the beck and call of the patient and a friendship would develop that is every bit as real as with another human. The easiest autonomous system would be to monitor and converse with the human without the need of actuators. These autonomous systems could maintain the bcEHR on the patient and notify stakeholders when an update has been made. Adding actuators to the autonomous system would allow for many other activities to be performed by the autonomous system. The autonomous system could help the human walk, ensure that wherever the human is siting that they are positioned correctly, and move them around a few times during the day and evening to ensure bed sores and other issues do not occur. The autonomous system could lift the human into or out of the toilet or bathroom and clean up after the human. The autonomous system could prepare food and in case of an emergency (fire, flooding, earthquake) stay with the human and possibly move them to safety.

Expanding the use of these robots beyond the elderly makes sense. It is difficult to determine how many people would need an autonomous system companion. An estimate of the number of humans that need physical assistance in the United States exceeds 20 million.[a] It is safe to say that a large number of people besides the elderly would benefit from an autonomous system companion. There are approximately 300,000 paraplegics and quadriplegics in the United States. These individuals need help to perform similar

[a]National Service Inclusion Project (2016) Basic facts: People with disabilities, http://www.serviceandinclusion.org/index.php?page=basic

daily functions that the elderly need. Mobility assistance, lifting them on or off toilets and tubs or beds, and rotating them at night as they sleep so they do not develop problems. The autonomous system companions also provide a way for their patients to interact with others whether that interaction is video or audio. These functions are not easy to implement and the investment needed to ensure an autonomous system companion can recognize the patient is in distress, determine the nature of the distress, figure out how to rectify the situation, and then execute the solution is extremely hard to implement for all the different ways a person needs to be lifted from the tub. Are they in need of being lifted from the tub because they are done with their bath or because in getting off the toilet they fell into the tub and in addition to getting the human to safety there is now a waste management problem to be solved?

A robot could also be attached to a person to provide them the ability to move around or with a prosthetic that replaces an arm or leg (bionics for real). The military is developing systems called exoskeletons that soldiers could wear to augment their performance.[6] They can run faster and jump higher! The same type of device could be outfitted to people who cannot move on their own or have great difficulty. The device would be an autonomous system on its own and provide services to the patient and caregivers associated with the patient. The exoskeleton can be considered an autonomous system companion in that it provides more than just mobile assistance. It can take data on the patient or at least connect to other devices on the human whether other prosthetics or IoTs inside the human. This version of the autonomous system companion could be told to take the human on a walk, to the store, or get them out of the flooded area and to the nearest medical facility. The autonomous system companion could sense if the person was in distress (e.g., a heart attack) and administer basic help while it took the person to a medical facility and communicated with the medical facility.

Any autonomous system companion could own or at least manage the bcEHR for an elderly person. It could provide information back to a doctor who can then instruct the robot to take some action like "make sure the patient drinks another 8 ounces of water a day" and record all these instructions in the bcEHR as well as inform the patient. The bcEHR can be used to manage the lifecycles of major events like a 2-week hospital stay for hip surgery including storing all of the opaque financial transactions. The bcEHR would be the integration point for all of the organizations associated with the patient to share access to their data and applications without compromising data security and integrity. The autonomous system companion should be able to notify stakeholders when events occur that are inserted into the bcEHR for the patient and take action based on those communications.

4. Print Me a New Heart While I Wait

Heart valve replacements are about as rote a procedure as one can imagine though in reading many web sites of hospitals that do them, one would be led to believe that they are still akin to open heart surgery. A leading indicator of how rote processes can begin dealing with even the most life-threatening conditions can be seen with heart valve replacements using a new non-invasive procedure.[7] The Transcatheter Aortic Valve Replacement (TAVR) procedure is used to insert a new heart valve using a catheter. Today a replacement valve can be a mechanical device or a valve made from the heart of a pig or cow. These mechanical valves are not complicated and can now be printed.

There is active research into the 3D printing of biocompatible materials, cells, and supporting components into complex 3D functional living tissues.[8] Of equivalent value though are parts of organs which if replaced could solve the problem. Heart valves are one example. Other organs, like the kidneys and stomach, do not need a full replacement to solve problems. Replacing just part of an organ with a printed replacement would suffice to solve the problem. In general, there are four categories of 3D organ printing: 2D tissues such as skin; hollow tubes such as blood vessels; hollow non-tubular organs such as the bladder; and complete organs such as the stomach. Expectation is again for the bottom-up approach. 2D printing should mature faster than hollow tubes, which should mature faster than hollow non-tubular organs, which should mature faster than a complete organ.

This section shows that the use of 3D medical printing is possible and usable by healthcare autonomous system. At the advanced edge of this process is to print IoTs onto the biological component being printed. The 3D printer could naturally insert a small IoT into the skin, blood vessel, bladder, or organ to help monitor the condition of the component over time. This IoT could then connect to an autonomous system companion or other external device to allow the content generated to be used by first responders.

5. Autonomous Surgery

The appeal of having an autonomous system operate on humans is undeniable. The current state of the art is the Intuitive Surgical's da Vinci surgical robot platform which is a master–slave system under control of the surgeon and not autonomous. The obvious appeal is that autonomous systems trained specifically to do a certain surgery can do them 24 by 7 by 365. People needing this procedure could be queued up and sent through the surgery and then to recovery on a much more predictable schedule. Safety would be another benefit of these machines as the work would get done the same way each time for each patient. The question to the machine would no longer be "how many of these do you do a week?" or "where is your degree from?" Presumably, the machine is outfitted with algorithms based on the best practices of surgeons everywhere. Another appeal of surgical autonomous systems is cost in that the cost of the autonomous system to hospitals can be amortized over many thousands of patients using leasing or other creative financing. There would no longer be a cost for the surgical team. The cost would be the cost to use the machine for a few hours.

The metaphor of an assembly line is an unfortunate one yet it is apropos. The introductory discussion about an entire practice and building optimized to handle hip and knee replacements is missing this one component to make it more autonomous, namely autonomous systems optimized to do knee and hip replacement surgery. There are other common surgeries that are amenable to such as business model. Imagine a hospital not as some large monolithic building but building optimized for certain procedures.

The cost for these procedures lend themselves well to new approaches. The cost of the surgical autonomous systems could be a simple leasing arrangement between the hospital and the vendor. It could also include someone leasing the autonomous system to the hospital and in return the hospital provides them space and the machine can invoice the patient or patient healthcare provider. The surgical autonomous system could interact with the patient's blockchain of medical information to use as part of the procedure.

There are two challenges to any surgical autonomous system: computer vision and algorithms that can execute complex surgical tasks. Computer vision is a very healthy area of research[9] and we will not discuss it here. Suffice it to say that it enables actionable information to be derived from images and video captured by a very sophisticated IoT that simulates human and animal vision. Algorithms to perform the surgical tasks is a maturing field within the robotics research area. The challenge for surgical autonomous system is the same for researchers trying to develop robotics to handle complex tasks like those for a physical therapist. The first challenge here is to be able to identify what it is looking at once an incision is made, assuming the surgical autonomous system knows where to perform the incision and make it deep enough.[b] It takes a few minutes to get a clear view of the organs and then unambiguously identify what is in front of it. There then needs to be a recognition of exactly what it is seeing. Is it looking at the appendix or do some organs need to be manipulated gently to expose it? We could go on and on articulating each step and watching a video of a procedure shows the clear challenges an surgical autonomous system would face even with the simplest operation.

---

[b] The authors suggest the reader watch a surgical video from youtube.com to get a better understanding of the challenges to a surgical autonomous system once the initial incision is made.

The constant monitoring of a patient could also be done by the surgical autonomous system. In principle, the autonomous system could apply the anesthesia and monitor the patient reaction during the operation to modulate the drugs uses so that only a minimal amount is being applied. The physical state of the patient could also be monitored and stored on the patient blockchain. The blockchain would be capturing the entirety of the operation including the patient's state.[c] In case of patient difficulty during the operation, the surgical autonomous system should be able to sense the problem or problems faster than a human would. The surgical autonomous system could take corrective action rapidly and the problem might be over in seconds rather than minutes if the patient was depending on humans to execute that Observe-Orient-Decide-Act phase. A machine has the ability to execute that phase faster than even the human as organs can begin to deteriorate and it would have greater value to the patient than any surgeon.

There is no lack of effort to create surgical autonomous systems.[10] A recently published paper demonstrates how an autonomous system is able to suture the intestines of a pig. One might think this is a simple thing and it is. A vet can do this in about 8 minutes. The surgical autonomous system described in the paper took about 50 minutes and was guided by a fluorescent dye to guide the actuators performing the suturing. And all the surgical autonomous system did was to suture just the incision in the pig's intestine. The machine did not anesthetize the pig nor did the machine perform the incision on the pig or the incision on its intestine or the final suturing to close the pig up. Most of this work was done by the research team. The surgical autonomous system was able to close the incision on the pig intestine. The research team performed measurements on the efficacy of the process and determined that the outcome of supervised autonomous procedures was superior to surgery performed by expert vets.

This one result provides a line of sight to how progress can be made to develop the whole autonomous system (AI + analytics +

---

[c] Useful also to lawyers who want to sue for malpractice, that is, if they could figure out who to sue when surgical autonomous systems are used.

IoT + actuators) to do precision surgery. Again, it appears progress comes incrementally. Currently approved surgical autonomous systems are not autonomous system but precision tools for surgery. It is clear that progress will be made as vision and algorithms to control the actuators improves over time. A probable future is that the more functionality accreted by surgical autonomous system the less the surgeon will do. This dynamic parallels what is occurring in the aviation field where the pilot is truly doing less and less and the autonomous system is doing more and more, regardless if passengers realize this. The use of surgical autonomous system on humans will not be so opaque. A person will know if they have the option of being operated on by a surgical autonomous system. The reflex reaction is that no way would a human want a robot operating on them regardless of its safety record and success rates. But as it is with commercial airlines where a person might want to go on a completely autonomous flight if they could do Chicago-Shanghai round trip for $149 and not $1499. People in pain or who do not want to wait 6 months for a hip replacement done by a human surgeon might very well opt for the surgical autonomous system, which could do it next week for substantially less cost to the patient.

The focus of attention on surgical autonomous systems is always on doing a specific operation well. There is more the surgical autonomous system can do besides that. Once an incision is made, it is possible for the surgical autonomous system to examine other parts of the patient's body in a non-invasive way while it is also performing the operation. Consider a simple appendectomy which removes the appendix that has no known use. An appendectomy is one of the most common procedures done but the sheer act of doing it allows for adjacent value-added actions to be taken. A small drone or fiber optic cable could be released into the colon to map the inside. This activity should take only a few minutes and yet would return valuable information on the state of an organ. This would be preferable for a patient over 50 who faced the uncomfortable prospects of having a colonoscopy done very few years. Why not take advantage of the situation to gather more data on a patient that should prove useful in the future? Colorectal cancer is the third leading cancer amongst men and women in the United States. If the drone or fiber cable detects an area that is classified as possibly cancerous, it can take a sample for biopsy, perhaps even increasing the rate of early detection.

Another example is if surgery is done that exposes a vein or artery that goes directly to the heart. A popular technique is to insert a catheter into a vein or artery that moves to the heart to allow for a comprehensive examination of the heart and surrounding blood vessels. This process enables the physician to take angiograms, record blood flow, calculate cardiac output and vascular resistance, perform an endomyocardial biopsy, and evaluate the electrical activity of the heart. Suppose you are having a hernia operation in the groin area. This is another simple procedure that a surgical autonomous system could perform. This surgery has an adjacent opportunity to run a drone or catheter up the femoral artery to do an examination of the heart and return that information to the patient by including it in the patient blockchain. The procedure is not done until the typical symptoms that cause the over 3 million procedures to be done in the United States are apparent. This procedure also includes the use of an X-ray machine to guide the action of the doctor. It is possible the design of the surgical autonomous system catheter would not require the use of an X-ray machine because either the drone or catheter could communicate with the surgical autonomous system via wireless or Bluetooth. The appeal here is that if the hernia of a patient has to be fixed, why not do other diagnostics to capture information on the patient so they do not have to wait for chest pains, abnormal results from various tests, or some other leading indicator of a heart attack.

6. Autonomous Hospitals

The hospital will necessarily be an aggregator of autonomous system considering the different functions a hospital performs: diagnosing, testing, therapy, screening, consultations, interventions, procedures, rehabilitation, and patient monitoring are a few. This begs the question: Who is the customer of a hospital? It is never clear whether the customer is the patient, the person who is the primary on the health insurance coverage, or the health insurance company. Not being able to define the customer means that it is difficult to make the hospital autonomous. The nature of the customer tends to define and focus of the autonomous system, the data to be collected and processed, the decisions to be made, and the actions to be taken. Another layer of issues is prioritization. How would the various autonomous activities be prioritized by the autonomous system? A hospital can be viewed as producing the product for the health insurance company where the sick patient is the raw material and the cured patient is the end product. The health insurance company really wants patients who do not make claims but pay their premiums, either themselves or through their employer. If the patient makes claims then the health insurer wants the process to be done with minimal costs.

Therefore, it is useful to view a hospital as taking in raw materials, performing value-added work on the raw materials, and producing a product that meets the customer expectations. The question of interest to automation is this: Is the value-added work being done in a hospital rote and repeatable as an assembly line or are there many processes with each process being done differently in non-standard ways? The former is needed to consider how automated a hospital can become while the latter is an example of something that would be difficult to automate. Is there a way to integrate the two? A key difference between the knee procedure and someone walking into the ER with symptoms only is that the former has a definitive diagnosis and the latter does not. The diagnosis piece appears to be the most difficult to automate though this is not stopping significant sums of money being spent to automate it. We have concluded above that diagnosis is best done with the human + autonomous system rather than autonomous system only. Can it be expected that once the diagnosis is done that the rest of the procedures are rote? Not for 20% of the cases. There will always be patients whose problems transcend the use of any autonomous system no matter how good. This is because new problems will continually occur for which there is little or no legacy knowledge. How would an autonomous system deal with AIDS? Would it have recognized it as a spectrum of conditions caused by infection with the human immunodeficiency virus? It took several years for the medical community to recognize AIDS for what it is and even longer to develop drug therapies to treat the conditions. If there is little or no existing knowledge of new diseases, what will the autonomous system use to ascertain the underlying cause of symptoms? In fact, the autonomous system will not be able to and this reinforces the need for the human + autonomous system model at the front end of any condition, namely diagnosis. For purposes of our discussion, even tests and diagnostics for AIDS were finally developed, so at some point the hospital can move beyond diagnostics to treatments.

We first consider the assembly line paradigm. This paradigm is where the aforementioned knee surgery would fit. At some point in a patient lifecycle, a decision is made on what to do to the patient to resolve the situation. The prognosis should result in a well-defined workflow being developed and executed by the autonomous system with human assistance. It is at this point that rote processes, that is, processes that can be automated, begin. The role of the human at this point does not disappear, but more activities that are typically done by humans could now be done by autonomous system. For example, the management of information associated with the patient is entered in manually or via the various machines in use. It is possible with voice recognition, video surveillance, and other data collected around the patient that the autonomous system could control what is being done and ensure it gets done. This workflow can be owned and managed by the autonomous system and presumably, like has happened with traditional assembly lines, reduction of errors and consistency of practice should lead to better results and outcomes. The benefits of the traditional assembly line is that the final product was better, met expectations of the customer, and lowered the cost of creating the product.

A key input for an autonomous system would be video when coupled with any machines capturing information on the patient. Constant surveillance of patients even when they are in their room is not really possible now and could be with existing technology.

The video can be further enhanced if the video itself had filters optimized for certain conditions. For example, a camera can be fitted with a 10 micron filter which is the wavelength that humans or other mammals emit most of their radiation. Any changes to the temperature of the human could be confirmed with a temperature sensor as well. Bleeding from some location would appear instantly on a body. A patient that was fine and then started to become distressed can be identified as such on a video and the autonomous system could take action as long as it was trained to recognize this sort of behavior. If the camera was a hyperspectral one it could monitor the patient at many different wavelengths simultaneously. Given the wide angle field of view, the hyperspectral camera could monitor not just the patient but also all of the machines and surfaces in the room for bacteriological contamination.[11,12] Bacteria exist in biofilm form which are organized communities of bacteria living in polymeric forms. Biofilms can form on various surfaces such as catheters, contact lenses, and the medical devices used to monitor a patient. According to a National Institute of Health estimation, 80% of human infections can be related to biofilm.[d] Hyperspectral imaging of a patient room, the equipment in the room, and the patient will allow as autonomous system to ensure the patient is progressing according to expected recovery parameters and not being put in danger of contracting an infection.

A constant monitoring of patients in this way would allow a series of autonomous system to be matured to handle specific patients. Just like the assembly lines that produce cars are different from the assembly lines that produce aircraft, it is expected that the same is true of patients with different conditions. The attribute of a hospital is that it has the equivalent of inventory turnover that is rapid enough that an autonomous system could be trained to increasing levels of maturity over time for the different types of patients. People of different ages, sex, and backgrounds

---

[d] Department of Health and Human Services, Immunology of biofilms, http://grants. nih.gov/grants/guide/pa-files/PA-07-288.html

will have different processes even if they are getting the same procedures.

An autonomous hospital should also benefit from the maturity of driverless cars and apply that knowledge to wheelchairs, hospital beds, and the various machines in the hospital. These can move themselves around and move patients around with little or no human assistance. The transfer of a patient from a bed or wheelchair to an MRI now requires the use of a human and in the future could use a robot or perhaps a wheelchair that could place the patient on the X-ray table. The autonomous systems can interact with one another and even charge to do its work with each transaction recorded in the bcEHR that manages the patient information and billing.

The use of the assembly line paradigm, however inappropriate it might seem to suggest people are products, has the utility of providing insights into the path to greater automation at a hospital. Hospitals would have to slowly build autonomy from the ground up and integrate the various autonomous systems, whether they be surgical autonomous system or a wheelchair, into overall processes. The bcEHR can be used to record each thing that happens to a patient or what each device does as well.

7. The Impact of Autonomous Healthcare

We have discussed automation of the healthcare industry. A seminal event that would greatly enhance healthcare delivery would be if humans owned their heath data and carried it with them at all times. Right now, humans have no ownership over the data collected about them from the various medical businesses we interact with over time. Enabling humans to carry their health data with them is not a technology issue; it is a policy issue. It is simple enough for people to carry around all of their financial information especially in a blockchain (Table 10.1).[e]

---

[e] Software like Quicken can aggregate all of your finances into a single file including tax information.

Table 10.1: Opportunities for big data in healthcare.

New Capabilities	As Is Analysis	Management Horizon	Strategic Horizon
System of Engagement	• Pilot M2M Transactions	• New end user device management (e.g., telepresence robots) • Operationalize M2M Transactions using blockchain	• Fully Autonomous
Diagnostics Surgery Hospitals Robo-Advisors	• Pilot Support of healthcare workers and patients	• autonomous system in surgery, ER, and other touch points between healthcare workers and between healthcare workers and patients • Breadth and Depth Enhancement of healthcare knowledge capital • Richer interactions with healthcare workers and patients	• Product Research • On-demand presence • Rich interactions with other autonomous system, humans
Blockchain Services	• Familiarization	• Pilot projects for use in basic processes and automation of internal manual processes	• Long-term monitoring by autonomous system of procedures and humans • Blockchain as the EHR • Transaction management

Medical businesses might find that allowing patients to have ownership over their data would mitigate their risks in a more automated delivery ecosystem. The more data the businesses own the more responsibility they have for the use and correctness of that data. Data makes them targets of cyberattacks. Data makes them spend more and more money to ensure a pristine amount of data for use in creating models. Let patients carry around the data, the IoTs that collect data on them, and the AI models that describe the patient. At the point of contact patients present this data to hospitals for their use. The onus is on the patient to provide their data and AI models in pristine conditions, not the hospital or medical practice that is seeing the patient. Automation opens up new opportunities around data governance and medical businesses would be wise to think creatively about the data governance process and their role in it.

A literature review of electronic health records (EHRs; there are many other designations such as Electronic Medical Records or EMRs. The differences are not germane to our discussions.) shows something very interesting. First, healthcare IT spend is about five times less than IT spending in financial services which tends to be at the leading edge. Second, and most telling, it is clear that the customer of the EHR software are hospitals, doctors, and insurance companies. No vendor seems to care whether individuals can access their information or not.

The change to the healthcare business model should originate with the maturation of the IoT and the systematic development of subject matter expertise that can be leveraged by a human or autonomous system agent. It is difficult to develop scenarios for fully autonomous hospitals since medical knowledge and device innovation are so rapid and pervasive. Healthcare is the nexus for how humans and autonomous systems will work best together. The humans can be surgeons, specialists, nurses, and billing trying to figure out the increasingly byzantine healthcare laws. The humans could also be cancer patients and their caregivers who need advice or just someone to talk to for a few minutes. A common pushback on autonomous systems in a healthcare setting is that they lack a bedside manner or the comfort provided by nurses and doctors. That complaint is a red herring as what people are probably saying is that they do not care how good autonomous systems are, they always want a human. Avatars can be very empathetic and learn how to interact over time with a human patient. This is also an area where robots can be used as companions or other human fulfillment needs. We anticipate a slow migration to Level 3.

References

1. Mathews, AW (24 April 2105). Anthem: Hacked database included 78.8 million people. *The Wall Street Journal.* http://www.wsj.com/articles/anthem-hacked-database-included-78-8-million-people-1424807364

2. Terhune, C (17 July 2015). UCLA Health System data breach affects 4.5 million patients. *Los Angeles Times.* http://www.latimes.com/business/la-fi-ucla-medical-data-20150717-story.html

3. Strömgren, AS, M Groenvold, A Sorensen and L Andersen (2001). Symptom recognition in advanced cancer. A comparison of nursing records against patient self-rating. *Acta Anaesthesiologica Scandinavica*, 45.

4. Robotic Trends (20 November 2015). Japan to create more user-friendly elderly care robots. http://www.roboticstrends.com/article/japan_to_create_more_user_friendly_elderly_care_robots/medical

5. Pew Research Center (21 May 2015). Family support in graying societies. http://www.pewsocialtrends.org/2015/05/21/family-support-in-graying-societies/

6. Science Alert (12 September 2014). New wearable robotic exoskeleton gives you superhuman powers. http://www.sciencealert.com/new-wearable-robotic-exoskeleton-gives-you-superhuman-powers

7. Kolata, G (20 June, 2015). Building a better value: A new approach to replacing narrowed heart valves allows older and sicker patients to survive treatment. *The New York Times.* http://www.nytimes.com/2015/06/22/health/heart-failure-aortic-valve-disease-tavr.html?_r=0

8. Sean, VM and A Atala (8 August 2014). 3D Bioprinting of tissues and organs. *Nature Biotechnology*, 32(8).

9. Reinhard K (2014). *Concise Computer Vision.* Berlin: Springer.

10. Shademan, A, RS Decker, JD Opfermann, S Leonard, A Krieger, and PCW. Kim (2016). Supervised autonomous robotic soft tissue surgery. *Science Translational Medicine*, 8, 337ra64.

11. Hanh ND. Le, *et al.* (2014). An average enumeration method of hyperspectral imaging data for quantitative evaluation of medical device surface contamination. *Biomedical Optics Express*, 5(10), 3613–3627.

12. Jun, W, MS Kim, K Lee, P Millner, and K Chao (2009). Assessment of bacterial biofilm on stainless steel by hyperspectral fluorescence imaging. *Sensing and Instrumentation Food Quality and Safety*, 3(1), 41–48. doi: 10.1007/s11694-009-9069-1.

CHAPTER 11

Speculations

1. Introduction

The future arrives in different places at different times. The evolution of autonomous systems will be accretive in nature with some areas becoming more automated than others faster and with immediate impact. There will be issues like aerial drones crashing into a crowd or an autonomous vehicle careening off a bridge with its passengers because it did not want to hit the school bus in front of it. The presence of autonomous systems dominating our lives will be implicit to most humans as evidenced today with some car and airplane components acting autonomously, unknown to humans. As autonomous systems begin to take over more mission-critical processes, their presence and impact will become more apparent. Their impact will show up in impacts to the workforce both in number and in the type of jobs humans would fill. One question is how governments will react when most transactions are M2M, no one drives a car, no one works in a restaurant, patients take medical advice from an avatar, or one of the other myriad of changes coming in the next 30 years. The blockchain can clearly be used for secure electronic voting but will the government allow that? The use of drones is accelerating and the FAA is moving forward with processes and regulatory framework to allow for drones while maintaining the integrity and safety of the US airspace. But are government processes in danger of being rendered irrelevant by autonomous system? How will the governments at all levels react to this societal transformation?

2. Rise of the Platforms

The enterprise architecture of businesses and of our own personal lives is becoming more of platform subscriptions to satisfy needs and requirements rather than purchase of or custom development of traditional software applications. The upside to this are more benefits that have been experienced to date with Facebook, Google, and LinkedIn. The downside is that businesses and humans no longer own these platforms and are at the mercy of how the platform providers allow access. The biggest downside is that no one, not even the platform owners, know and understand how people and AS will use their platforms in the future.

What is a platform? Platforms are entities like autonomous systems that provide capabilities that business and humans use as is or can customize or extend as they desire. Self-driving cars are platforms as is Facebook and LinkedIn. Humans are migrating away from anything resembling Windows and using mobile devices that provide everything they need without knowing or understanding the underlying operating system or other traditional applications.

The biggest weakness is that the owners of platforms truly do not know how business and humans will use the platforms. This is clearly evident in the use of Facebook and other platforms, the rise of "fake news", the publication of horrific videos showing suicide and killings in real time, and the manipulation of online ads and other online artifacts to influence election results. Platform providers are mistaken in the belief that they understand their platforms fully. They do not have a complete inventory of all uses cases for their platforms and the use cases that articulate cross-platform processes. This gap is a problem not just for the companies, but for humans, companies, and the government. The gap represents a problem for law enforcement and regulatory bodies because regulatory frameworks do not address these use cases.

The broader impact to humans and companies is how certain platforms will lock them in. Take for example Amazon. Amazon controls almost 50% of all U.S. e-commerce sales and over a third of holiday sales in 2017. Online retailers do not have much choice if they expect to scale their businesses. Go Amazon or go home. Salesforce, Amazon AWS, Windows Azure, Facebook, LinkedIn, and Google also have locked in humans and companies onto platforms that will prove to be very difficult to transition off of and onto new competitor platforms. This high bar to leaving is intentional and will become even more difficult in the future with autonomous systems. Once a company is in a supply chain with one or a handful of blockchains, how easy will it be for that company to leave that supply chain? They cannot take their piece of the blockchain with them. Their autonomous systems are optimized for that supply chain. The cost to leaving will escalate to the point where leaving is not an option and the barrier to entry is also huge. Why would a partner in the supply chain allow a competitor to join? This lock-in will stifle innovation and the creative destruction process.

The lock into platforms will get worse with time. Platforms are being deployed to host machine learning capabilities (e.g., h20.ai) and IoT software platforms (e.g., Predix). There is an ongoing attempt by Google, IBM, and many other companies to corner the market on the best data to use for creating AS. There is precedent for this locking. Companies had not considered themselves locked into ERP systems such as SAP or PeopleSoft for financials, HR, and supply chain. They soon discovered that once the ERP decision was made they could not switch. Acquisitions made this lock-in more permanent as most acquisitions left legacy systems in place. Migration to new ERPs was time-consuming and very expensive. And how long have companies used ADP or Bloomberg Terminals? There have been many opportunities to switch.

The AS for companies will become the new legacy. All these AS capabilities will be built on one or more previous versions of an attempt to replace older applications. A skeleton in almost every company closet is that most are still running systems written in the 1960s to do some task. Multiple replacement attempts over the years typically replaced part of a legacy system but not all of it. The result was that company applications are actually stacks with each level in the stack representing an attempt to replace what was below it. These legacy apps contain multiple architecture generations (mainframe, client/server, object oriented distributed servers, Internet, thick service layers, service brokers, and who knows what else).

These application stacks are actually very important. They encapsulate some key domain knowledge for a company. The AS suite developed for a company will need to access the data and processes inherent in those legacy apps. They are the crown jewels for most companies and will be needed if a company is going to differentiate itself from it peers with its new AS layer. This is at least one advantage that companies will have over the platform providers. The latter cannot offer data that is encapsulated at companies. The companies will have to securely use this data to enrich the data that is available from platform providers to develop new products and enter new markets.

3. Process Integration Points as Leading Indicators

What should we look for to see if autonomous systems are starting to make their way into our lives and business in a much more intrusive manner? It can be difficult to see inside companies to understand the extent of their use of autonomous system. Mining is easy but financial services is not. The best place to look for significant transformation to autonomous system is at those points of intersection in a supply chain or similar major business process. Consider the autonomous food supply. Regardless of how automated a farm is, this automation while independent of other industries, will still have to deal with an autonomous logistics company. How well does that integration work? Are the autonomous systems on the farm able to interact with the autonomous system logistic services? Can the autonomous system negotiate a good deal? Can the autonomous farm decide when to sell its crop and pay the Trone that moves it to get a better deal if it wants and split the proceeds? Does the crop get to its intended location and shipped to the right places? Once these results are evident then we can be assured that our society is becoming more automated and that the autonomous system is maturing.

We believe logistics will be the area where much of the autonomy is proven out and matured before it is used in areas where human lives depend on its safe operations. A leading indicator will be when a large delivery service like FedEx or UPS begins flying unmanned cargo planes like a 747. Another indicator will be when Amazon and others truly start and scale up delivery by drones and these become a mundane delivery channel that people do not notice.

Healthcare will be another area that will start to show first, we believe, how humans and autonomous system interact to deliver a mission-critical service, especially in the diagnostic field where a healthcare worker interacts with an autonomous system in the same manner as they would another human. No longer would you hear "Viv, what does it mean if a headache and nausea occur in a child who was in an auto accident?" Think about conversations a human has with a healthcare worker when discussing a child's condition. It is more back and forth than Q&A. A leading indicator here will be when a conversation with Viv or Cortana is conversational and not Q&A.

Another leading indicator of autonomous system maturity is when the government decides to step in and try to address the unintended consequences of autonomous system maturity. This is a sure sign that our lives are changing and that while good, bad, and ugly is happening, there is no going back.

4. Workforce Impact

A flash point for the discussion of autonomous system is the loss of jobs of humans. We have discussed this above in a number of sections and this topic is big among those people who appear on TV and at media-rich places like Davos. Discussing the threats of massive jobs loss and insurrections that would most certainly follow are not going to advance the thinking of the impact of autonomous system on our society. There is a common theme to previous industrial revolutions and the topic of autonomous system maturity might rise to that level. The theme is one of adaptation. Over time people did lose jobs and suffer. Out of this suffering came government policies that were well-intentioned but in the end, not of much value. What was of value were innovations that people created out of perceived needs. Labor unions were one innovation to help workers and new jobs that were not even imagined prior to the revolution were created. Workers were hired to support the new machines and run them. Yes, some resisted and revolted but most over time were able to adapt and this idea of adaptation was passed down to their children so that as the industrial revolutions played out, so do the adaptation.

We feel that in the future humans will adapt to the transformation in ways that are at this point, difficult to articulate. We believe a key area of employment growth will be when a human partners with an autonomous system to form a value generation nexus. The intuition of a human and the ability of an autonomous system to search and aggregate significant amounts of information will lead to new jobs being created that were heretofore not possible. There will be those who try to enforce an adaptation on the population and just as in the past, these prescriptive measures will probably fail. Some of the most amazing innovations were born out of the rubble of depressions, recessions, and major conflict as well as black swan events. We cannot predict a black swan event and prepare for it. What we can do is to try to identify it, watch it play out, and prepare for its full evolution.

5. Government Impact

For those who believe in big government and in strong regulatory frameworks to control large parts of the economy, the presence of autonomous system is a godsend. A key characteristic of automated processes is that the government could, if it so chose, to monitor what is going on and regulate it if it so deems at a very granular level. Consider automated farming operations. It would be possible for governments to manage autonomous farms by determining what farms in what areas grew what crops. It could then monitor crop production and determine where to send the output from each farm by controlling the automated trucks or trones that deliver the crops. It could tell the autonomous farms to stop growing crops in mid-season if it felt the production was going to be too high in one state to help the two senators from a larger corn-growing state who felt that the prices would disadvantage their farmers. The government, in adhering to the various climate agreements agreed to globally, might reduce cattle and pig inventories throughout the southeast to meet a level of greenhouse gas emissions demanded by some international NGO. There is also the possibility that supranational groups such as the EU could demand changes to US food production. In short, a society that is run largely by autonomous system could be managed by central authorities at the state and federal levels and even possibly by supranational groups. Is this scenario reasonable and desirable?

The growth of government is undeniable. The Code of Federal Regulations (CFR) is the codification of all rules and regulations promulgated by federal agencies. Its size has grown from under 25,000 pages in 1960 to over 175,000 at the end of 2014.[a] The Bible is about 1300 pages long, so today the CFR is the equivalent of a stack of 135 Bibles. The Federal Government is seeking to expand its reach to manage more land by using the Clean Water Act.[1] The EPA says it is only trying to clarify a law and not gain further control of waterways policy. Congress says the EPA is seeking to assert federal control over puddles, ditches, areas that are occasionally wet and other large sections of private or state land. The Endangered Species Act has been used to protect the Delta Smelt in California. Federal Authorities have diverted freshwater away from the San Joaquin Valley and drought-stricken farms to save the fish, in vain.[2] The extinction of the fish is all but certain; some say the same of the farms in the San Joaquin Valley.[3]

---

[a] Regulatory Studies Center, Columbian College of Arts & Sciences, The George Washington University, Reg Stats, 2016, https://regulatorystudies.columbian.gwu.edu/reg-stats.

There is a growing movement to provide a Universal Basic Income (UBI)[4] to all Americans.[b] This idea has been around for many years in many forms and has recently gained traction due to discussions around people losing their jobs to autonomous system. The idea is to give every person a basic income to provide a safety net and allow them to pursue other activities. Some pilots of this idea started in Canada with serious thought being given to doing pilots in the UK. Switzerland has a referendum to implement UBI fully. UBI in the United States. is not yet on the horizon but people are actively pursuing it. While autonomous system might be the cause of the employment disruption that is providing justification to a UBI, the autonomous system could just as easily serve as mechanisms for the government to expand beyond UBI and provide Universal Goods and Services (UGS). Consider fresh fruit like apples. It would be possible for an automated apple farm to have its crops taken in trones to a central facility where packages of small apples could be created. These packages could then be taken by small drones to people, in a manner similar to what Amazon is doing. Autonomous systems allow the government to provide benefits to people that are above and beyond just money. The government could provide food and other services to its citizens. Regardless of how people feel about these issues, it is clear that autonomous system will force a discussion in these areas whether we want to have these discussions or not.

6. Real Estate

The existence of AS, especially self-driving cars, will have a significant impact to real estate. A simple example will do. Los Angeles has about 200 square miles of parking lots. If most cars in Los Angeles are self-driving then there will be a reduced need to park them for the day. They can be repurposed during the day to carry humans, machines, products like groceries, or be serviced. The

---

[b] Basic Income Earth Network, About Basic Income, http://www.basicincome.org/basic-income/

introduction of this much space to the Los Angeles real estate market has housing and business implications. What would the city do with all that space? Use it for housing, business, or agriculture? The rise of vertical farming and its ability to start feeding large numbers of humans provides Los Angeles with an opportunity to zone these areas for vertical farming only, providing new jobs, tax revenues, and sustainable sources of food. Affordable housing for blue collar jobs is almost non-existent for most who are new to working in Los Angeles. Would this much land be made available for those who cannot currently afford housing? This is one area we expect many unanticipated things to happen with the introduction of AS.

7. Ownership of Autonomous Systems

Who will end up owning autonomous systems? It has always been the case that whenever something is to be owned, it is owned by a human or a company. A fleet of cars used for taxi services is owned by the taxi company, the drivers, or companies who lease the taxis to the taxi company. But there is no reason that now, with self-driving cars, that they cannot own themselves.

Consider a self-driving car that is used for taxi services. A variety of apps enables it to interact with a human or group of humans. The apps allows the human to summon the car, tell it where it wants to go, and completes payments. It can obtain fuel and maintenance services with a service station or dealerships. It can pay its taxes online. It can even have an accountant and lawyer because it just needs to provide the data these services requires.

Self-driving cars will need to be interrogated for their actions especially if they are in an accident or are being audited by government officials. The black box solution used in aircraft is an obvious solution though the information captured by the black box must be enhanced. The autonomous system needs to provide information on not just the decision made but why the decision was made. For a car, this must be in the context of existing transportation laws.

8. Quantum Computing

Quantum computing is the most esoteric concept that business leaders need a basic understanding of their capabilities. Bill Gates latest answer to an interviewer on quantum computing is a propos:

"I smiled when you suggested we should try to explain quantum [computing]. That's the one part of Microsoft where they put up slides that I truly do not understand. I know a lot of physics and a lot of math. But the one place where they put up slides and it is hieroglyphics, it's quantum [computing]."[5]

Business leaders and humans in general understand very little of the technologies they use. People use apps all the time with no understanding of the underlying technologies that make up the apps, the mobile phone, the wi-fi communications, and the cloud. What they do care about is having something that solves a problem for them while interacting in a common sense manner. So what kinds of problems can a quantum computer solve for business and humans?

A quantum computer uses quantum bits (qubits or qbits) to represent information. Traditional computers use a bit to represent information and a bit can have a value of 0 or 1. A qbit represents information using both a 0 and a 1 simultaneously. The implication is that a qbit can do two computations at once. Two qbits can each do two so that mean that two qbits can do four computations per second. Three qbits can do eight computations simultaneously. 50 qbits will do better than the best supercomputers in existence or likely to be in existence for quite some time. Building a quantum computer with 50 qbits that are shown to work is called quantum supremacy meaning that quantum computers will forever be better than digital computers.

There is a so what question here of course.

Enterprises should plan on quantum computers to be available as a platform from just a few providers.

Quantum computing does offer one major opportunity. The use of quantum computing by enterprises will result in many new kinds of jobs. These jobs should be in the area of how to enable business processes use quantum computing for operation of autonomous systems.

References

1. Cama, T (13 January 2016). House votes to overturn Obama water rule. *The Hill.* http://thehill.com/policy/energy-environment/265734-house-votes-to-overturn-obamas-water-rule

2. Kay, J (3 April 2015). Delta Smelt, Icon of California Water Wars, Is Almost Extinct. *National Geographic.* http://news.nationalgeographic.com/2015/04/150403-smelt-california-bay-delta-extinction-endangered-species-drought-fish/

3. California's Man-Made Drought (2 September 2009). The Wall Street Journal. http://www.wsj.com/articles/SB10001424052970204731804574384731898375624

4. Rotman, D (11 March 2016). The Danger of the Universal Basic Income. *MIT Technology Review.* https://www.technologyreview.com/s/601019/the-danger-of-the-universal-basic-income/

5. Stevensen, S (25 Sept 2017), "A Rare Joint Interview with Microsoft CEO Satya Nadella and Bill Gates", The Wall Street Journal, https://www.wsj.com/articles/a-rare-joint-interview-with-microsoft-ceo-satya-nadella-and-bill-gates-1506358852